21ST CENTURY
WICCA

21st Century Wicca

A Young Witch's Guide to Living the Magical Life

Jennifer Hunter

A Citadel Press Book
Published by Carol Publishing Group

Carol Publishing Group Edition, 1999

A Citadel Press Book
Published by Carol Publishing Group
Citadel Press is a registered trademark of Carol Communications, Inc.

Editorial, sales and distribution, and rights and permissions inquiries should be addressed to Carol Publishing Group, 120 Enterprise Avenue, Secaucus, N.J. 07094

In Canada: Canadian Manda Group, One Atlantic Avenue, Suite 105, Toronto, Ontario M6K 3E7

Carol Publishing Group books may be purchased in bulk at special discounts for sales promotion, fund-raising, or educational purposes. Special editions can be created to specifications. For details, contact: Special Sales Department, Carol Publishing Group, 120 Enterprise Avenue, Secaucus, N.J. 07094.

Chapter heading illustrations by Ariel Kornblit, all other interior illustrations and photographs by Jennifer Hunter.

Manufactured in the United States of America
10 9 8 7 6 5 4

Library of Congress Cataloging-in-Publication Data

Hunter, Jennifer.
    21st century Wicca : a young witch's guide to living the magical life / Jennifer Hunter.
        p.   cm.
    "A Citadel Press book."
    Includes bibliographical references.
    ISBN 0-8065-1887-1 (pbk.)
    1. Witchcraft. 2. Spritual life. 3. Hunter, Jennifer. I. Title.
    BF1566.H846 1997
    133.4'3—dc21
                                                                    97-8640
                                                                      CIP

To all my greatest teachers:

Bongo, Bryan, Judy Harrow, Orin Kornblit, David Lee, Mom,
Jenny Moon, Mrs. Rice, Alex Shimoda.

And to the greatest teachers of all—
Who also give the hardest tests—
The Lord and Lady.

Contents

Preface

About This Book—and Some of the People in It

I wrote this book because I felt that most of the books on Wicca were giving us too much of what we didn't need: flowery rituals, tables of correspondences, complicated spells—and yet, virtually no information about the reasons behind all of that. Who were these deities we were calling on? What kind of mental state should you be in while you're crafting that spell? What does it really feel like to move energy around? And finally, how do we bring this magical sensibility into our daily lives?

In this book, I am more interested in talking about the "why" and "how" than the "what." There are dozens of books about different Wiccan traditions, and different takes on those traditions. This won't be one of them. Aside from my brief training in a Gardnerian coven (which, in its rituals, was pretty damn eclectic), I have been outside of any particular tradition for the nine years I've been practicing. I have never felt an affinity for a particular set of deities, symbols, or rituals. (I have recently given up trying to

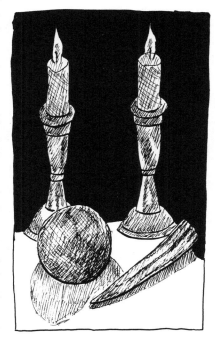

be Celtic and have started to work on developing a tradition that calls on *my* heritage, which is Jewish, but that's another book.) Instead, I have always focused on the common denominators: What symbols and rituals are shared by all these traditions? What are the basic beliefs of Wicca? How can I learn more about the truths that seem to be constant? And further, how does magic work? What is my idea of Deity? How can I take care of my magical energy?

There are those who believe that these things I talk about are meant to be studied only by experienced Witches who have already become comfortable with the trappings of their particular tradition. In crafts like painting or writing, it's good to have a rigid structure first, and only after we have mastered the rules can we progress to more heartfelt, creative work. However, Wicca-craft is not a skill, it is a spiritual path. Even those things within Wicca that require practice—writing rituals or learning how to meditate—must begin with the individual's focus, sense of purpose, and understanding of what she's doing. Otherwise we are only mouthing the words and following a script. What good is magic without spirit? Magical and spiritual practice must grow the natural way: from the roots up. If you eventually want to make your search specific to one tradition, you can get that from other books. And at least by then, you'll understand why you're doing all those things!

Another reason for this book: Magic too often becomes either a universal scapegoat or a universal problem-solver. I've seen people get pulled into "Faerieland" while their relationships, career, health, and personal development suffer. This, to me, is contrary to the whole point of magic. When we go "between the worlds," we are touching on a deeper level of reality than the physical world. However, this does not mean the magic we do should be isolated from the physical. Unless we are able to manifest that magical spark as real, positive change, it is useless. Sacred space is not a place to play make-believe, or to hide. In this book I explore ways to make magic happen on a real, tangible level— ways to birth it *through* the magic circle into your everyday life.

Besides, these two aspects of your life are interdependent. Just as you can do a spell to help you with your exams in college, so your happiness (or unhappiness) at school can affect your magical concentration. You are a whole person. If you are a Witch, you are no less a parent, student, daughter, son, musician, or soccer player. This book gives you accurate information about the philosophy, beliefs, and practice of Wicca, as well as practical, concrete ways to use that information throughout your entire life.

What you learn here will be useful to you, no matter if you have no idea what Wicca is, if you've already set your mind to follow that path, or if you're somewhere in between. There are parts that may explain things you already know, or that will seem obvious. Read the whole book anyway. Beginners will learn just as much about the Craft when they read about the practical, everyday aspects in the later chapters, as they will from the parts about the nuts and bolts of magic. Those who have been practicing for a while can use the basic, informative chapters as a reminder of what they may sometimes forget, and to help develop their own sense of the Craft—which should always be changing anyway.

I recommend that you at least try the exercises given in some of the chapters. They're there for a reason: They work. The exercises will show you in reality what the chapters discuss in theory. When I was learning the Craft on my own, I thought that just reading the books and gathering the knowledge was all I needed. But I soon discovered that reading about energy is a far cry from actually moving it around. Magic is not just a philosophy, it is a practice. And it *takes* practice!

The popular idea of magic is that all you need to do is get your hands on a certain book that will give you a a list of powerful ingredients and words. Just paint-by-the-numbers! Unfortunately, some "spell books" on the market today help to strengthen this idea. The spells in these books may be beautifully written and carefully researched, but they are nothing on their own. The words and images only provide a focus for *you* to work the magic. To suggest otherwise would be like saying that the canvas, brushes, and paints could themselves create a masterpiece.

This book does include instructions on how to put together an effective spell. But if you are just starting in the Craft, I strongly warn against skipping directly to that section. That would be like a sixteen year old trying to drive a car cross-country before learning how to drive. She might not even get it to start, but if she does, she runs the very great risk of getting into an accident. Magic isn't safe, but it can be practiced safely.

You will often hear people speak of the Mysteries of the Craft. That seems to imply that some bit of knowledge will be handed to you when you get to a certain level of training. Certainly all traditions and many covens have their secrets, but it's important to know the difference between secrets and Mysteries. Secrets can be given away. I don't know what happens in the third-degree initiation in the Gardnerian tradition, because I do not have access to that text. Parts of some traditions' rituals were meant to be secret, but then someone decided to publish them.

Mysteries, on the other hand, must be directly experienced. When you read, you are operating on an intellectual level. You may objectively understand the idea, "thou art God," but there's a big difference between believing it and living it. This book cannot hand you a Mystery. No book can, and no High Priestess can. The only things that have value are those which you have found out for yourself.

The People in This Book

I interviewed several Pagans and Witches I knew, in order to give the book the feel of a workshop at a Pagan festival. This is so you'll feel that you are in good company, and you will also have the chance to learn from your friends in the community—not just from the one who's running the meeting!

AUTUMN is twenty-eight years old and lives in Pennsylvania. She sells gemstones at Pagan festivals and is often very busy taking care of her four-year-old son.

BLAIR is a twenty-year-old college student from Bridgeton, New Jersey, who has been studying the Craft for about four years. He started in a Dianic coven and is now studying Bluestar Traditional Wicca with Barley Moon Coven in the New Brunswick, New Jersey area.

CATHERINE is a thirty-seven-year-old herbalist, writer, and businesswoman, who lives in Newark with her three-year-old son,

Justin. She loves to work in her garden and says it's part of her Craft on many levels.

KRISTINE is a twenty-eight-year-old administrative assistant who lives in New Jersey. She's loves rocks and crystals, exercising, reading and writing, staring at the moon, horseback riding, living a modest life, and applying her learnings.

DAVID is thirty-three years old, lives in Franconia, Pennsylvania, and works in management for a manufacturing company. He has been practicing Wicca as a solitary since high school and is very active in the environmental protection movement.

JAKE is a twenty-five-year-old musician and music teacher. She is ex-lead singer of the group Evelyn Situation. An east-coaster transplanted to the Southwest, she's into theater, songwriting, and is a sometime radio DJ.

JENNE is a twenty-one-year-old graduate student, studying English literature at Drew University. She is a solitary eclectic Witch whose writings have appeared in *Circle Network News* under the name "Morrigan-Aa." She is also a published poet.

JUDY is fifty-one years old and lives in New York City. She has been practicing the Craft for twenty years. She has held various offices in Covenant of the Goddess and was the first member of CoG to be legally registered as clergy in New York City. Judy is High Priestess of Proteus Coven and founder of the Protean Tradition. Her essays can be found in the second and third of Chas Clifton's *Witchcraft Today* anthologies.

KAREN is a twenty-six-year-old office worker, studying to be a certified massage therapist. She moved to central New Jersey from England a couple of years ago. She does Reiki, and working with energy on a regular basis has become a "big deal" in her life. She reads a lot, particularly about Celtic and Germanic mythology.

KERRI is a twenty-eight-year-old school bus driver who lives in Connecticut with her husband and three children. She is a member of two covens, one Celtic and one eclectic Wiccan. She loves to sew and has too many dogs, cats, and ferrets to mention.

Kerri, with her family.

LAUREL is thirty years old and lives in Central New Jersey. She is a professional vocalist who works in local church parishes as choir director, cantor, and soloist. She has been involved in the Craft for about ten years, five years eclectic, five years Gardnerian. She is well-known in the community for her original Pagan music under the pen name of "Siren."

LORRIE, a thirty-year-old homemaker, has been practicing Celtic and Wiccan traditions for almost thirteen years. She lives with her husband and three children in the Pocono Mountains of Pennsylvania. They are a Wiccan family.

MARGOT is thirty-four years old and lives in Sussex County, New Jersey. She is a writer, reverend, and mother; and deems all three of equal importance. She is a "starets," which is an Eastern European shaman who follows an ecumenical tradition. She enjoys doing sacred needlework.

MEILIKKI is a twenty-six-year-old Pagan student who lives in Southern New Jersey. She likes to go to the gym to work out and surfs the Net in her spare time (like she has spare time).

MISHA is forty-year-old self-described "generic Pagan" who lives in Doylestown, Pennsylvania. He's a market researcher as a vocation, but a writer, singer, composer, and equestrian as an avocation.

OBSIDIANA is thirty-eight years old, lives in Central New Jersey, and considers herself "your basic eclectic solitary." To keep her creditors happy she makes electronic "stuff." To keep herself happy she makes music, and arts-and-crafts "stuff."

RAINBOW DARKLY is a thirty-two-year-old mail-handler for the postal service who lives in upstate New York. She has been dedicated to the Craft for almost fourteen years, and is a member of two Wiccan covens (one in hibernation), a kabbalistic lodge, and the Church of the Sacred Earth. She raises reptiles and lectures about them, gardens, camps, and does too much driving.

STEPHEN is a thirty-six-year-old carpenter who lives in North Arlington, New Jersey. He is also a psychic astrologer and priest. He enjoys dancing, drumming, and singing, and is the father of one very special two year old.

TOM is a twenty-five-year-old computer consultant who lives in Central New Jersey. He is very loosely affiliated with the Blue Star tradition and has some traditional background, but is mostly eclectic. He has used the I Ching for many years. In his spare time he likes to read and play computer games.

UGRIC is thirty-nine years old and lives in Akron, Ohio. He is a tarot reader and clinical hypnotherapist, and he belongs to the Society for Creative Anachronism. He is an eclectic practitioner of Magick and a Native American traditionalist, and teaches both of these locally.

VICTORIA is a twenty-five-year-old massage therapist who lives in the southwestern United States. She is currently working on her second degree in an eclectic Wiccan tradition. Her coven's recent focus has been the Goddess Brigid, to whom Victoria feels especially close because of their common interest in healing work.

PART ONE

The Maiden
The Roots of Wiccan Practice

We call on you, O Maiden
As she who cannot be tamed;
We hear your footsteps echo through the fields,
We hear the music of your laughter.
You, who are the beginning of beginnings,
You, who light the fire of the sun.
Bring to us the passion of your dancing,
Teach us to see with child's eyes.

CHAPTER ONE

Beginnings

What's This All About, Anyway?

Why would you pick up a book on Witchcraft? You may be looking for a sense of power, or for insight into the unknown. Maybe
you're not happy with "mainstream" religion and want to see what
your options are. Or maybe you want to learn how to use your
natural psychic abilities. Perhaps you want to become closer to
Nature. Maybe you've been practicing the Craft for some time and
want to learn more about your path. Or are you just curious?

> LAUREL: "I was a church-music major and had aspirations of
> being an exorcist. I wanted to study and find out what it was
> about. I was very interested in parapsychology and was going
> to courses, study groups, and support groups in the New Age
> community, mainly learning anything I could lay my hands
> on. But, of course, you discover that only men can be priests
> and therefore only they can be exorcists, and you, poor little
> Catholic girl, cannot do that. So we bagged that."

When you're motivated by curiosity and the desire to learn, any reason is a good one. The newcomer to Witchcraft usually has very little idea what it's all about. I certainly didn't, but when I learned what it was, I loved it all the more. I came to the Craft looking for power, but when I found it, it wasn't at all what I had expected. I came looking for mystery, and the Mysteries were grander than anything I could have imagined. I came looking for answers, and I found dozens of new questions—and now I understand that's as it should be.

KERRI: "When I was younger, I had never read any book on Wicca, I had no knowledge at all of what true Witches were, but I often found myself outside, staring at the moon, lighting incense around where I sat, in a circle. I spent a lot of time in the woods, and I felt more at peace in the woods by myself than with anyone I knew. When I started finding out things about Wicca, I found that many of the things that Wiccans feel and many of things they do in ritual, I had been doing for years without knowing."

KRISTINE: "I've always been drawn to some kind of magical existence, always felt that there was another plane within this plane. About a year and a half ago, somebody mentioned [the Craft] as something that was their religion, and I just went to the bookstore and bought $100 worth of books on Paganism, Wicca, Witchcraft. I didn't know which one to buy, so I bought all the ones that interested me at that moment. And I just started reading, reading, reading. Then I went onto America Online and went into the "Ask-a-Witch Room" and the "Pagan Teahouse," and I started chatting with people. Everyone was very friendly. They were very open to offering ideas and to giving me book titles that they thought would be a good place to start for me."

Few religious traditions are as misunderstood as Witchcraft. If you are unfamiliar with it, you may be surprised to learn that it is a religion at all. Also called "Wicca," or "the Craft," it takes its inspiration from the oldest known religions in Europe. The holidays, beliefs, magical traditions, and Gods are very similar to those of Pagan folk from long before the coming of Christianity.

However, the Old Religion did not survive intact. Between the years 300 and 1000 C.E. through preaching, politics, and often violence, the new religion all but demolished the old ways of the European people. It has been said that "the Gods of the old religion become the devils of the new." If you want to convert large numbers of people to your faith, it is not enough to show them what you believe. You must convince them that what they have believed is wrong. Over time, the old gods and the old ways were no longer seen as sacred, but rather, as the very definition of evil.

Pagan once meant "country-dweller." Heathen meant "one who dwells on the heath"—just another way of saying "out in the country." The folks who lived in out-of-the-way places were a little more resistant to religious conversion. *Pagan* and *heathen*, once simple statements of location, became insults, synonymous with someone who was backward and uncultured. A Pagan became either a barbarian with no religion, or someone whose religion was based on superstition and the bizarre.

It's difficult to trace the origins of the word *witch* as accurately as those of *pagan* and *heathen*. But it is certainly a cousin of theirs—it's a word from medieval times, used to describe anyone who refused to convert, who used magic, who was more powerful than perhaps she should have been. It was more often used for women, but there were men accused of witchcraft as well. *Witch* was probably an insult from the start, but it has been adopted proudly by those who feel kinship with those stubborn country-dwellers of medieval Europe.

With the coming of Christianity, the old religion was almost dead. It stayed that way for hundreds of years. But as in Nature, when things die, they return again in another form. And this is no exception. In the 1930s an inventive and inspired English man named Gerald Gardner sincerely wanted to bring back the old ways of his native land. He borrowed from Jewish mysticism, from ceremonial magic, from British folklore and tradition, and from historians such as Margaret Murray (the *Witch-Cult of Western Europe* and *God of the Witches*) and Sir James Frazer (*The*

Golden Bough). He then added a bit from his imagination and created the first form of the religion that is now called Wicca, or Witchcraft.

Gardner had people believe that Wicca was an ancient religion and that the magical documents in his posession had been passed down to him by an unbroken lineage of Wiccans. Most of the sources from which Gardner was working were certainly ancient, but all evidence points to the fact that the Wicca he practiced was his creation. Gardner was initiated into an existing coven, but very little is known about what tradition that was—it may or may not have been similar to modern Wicca.

Since Gardner passed away in the 1960s we can't ask him, so we don't know this for certain, but almost all the text of his magical compendium, or Book of Shadows, has been traced to various other sources (read *Crafting the Art of Magic*, by Aidan Kelly, for a more detailed explanation). Since people have begun taking a closer look at Gardner's work, the question of the history of Witchcraft seems to plague the community more and more. Some say Gardner made it all up; some say he had ancient sources; some say they themselves practice a Stone Age religion that never went through Gardner. And some use their historical claims to say that they are the only "true Witches."

The sad part is that none of this really matters. All great religions have to start somewhere. And even if Wicca were as old as Gardner claimed, it couldn't possibly remain the same as it was originally. Times have changed. The important part is that the old truths, the roots, remain the same. They survive because they are timeless, linked into Nature, the unity of all things, and the joy and wonder of life.

KAREN: "I think there has been a tendency for people to talk about the 'Burning Times' (a semi-mythical period of Witch persecutions)—and the whole idea of traditions being handed down unbroken for centuries. I think that is a load of shit. But shit is good fertilizer. It's kind of a nice fantasy to believe that's what happened. I think perhaps it did in a few rare cases, but I don't think we should have any illusions. Modern Paganism and modern Craft are basically the modern interpretation of ancient myths and ancient ways of doing things."

So, what Gardner began, the rest of us continue. Witchcraft is a religion created by those who practice it. Therefore, it stays diverse and is constantly evolving. While some covens trace their lineage in an unbroken line back to Gardner, the majority of Witches today are those who pick up a book or two and begin practicing on their own. These people are reinventing the old traditions, drawing inspiration from those who went before—and from themselves. In other words, they are doing just what Gerald Gardner originally did.

There is a broader spectrum of "Neo-Paganism," which includes all the various traditions of Wicca, some other forms of folk magic and Witchcraft, Native American shamanism, Goddess worship, ceremonial magic, and many other traditions. It is much harder to define Neo-Paganism than it is to define Witchcraft, because it is so diverse. Neo-Pagans will agree on the basic sacredness of life and on the fact that each of us is responsible for the effect of our actions on the rest of the world. There *are* people who identify as Pagan and not Wiccan. In this book I use the terms Wiccan and Pagan pretty much interchangeably, because that's how they are often used in the community. As you read and study more, you'll probably decide upon your own distinctions between the two.

Basic Wiccan Beliefs

1. THERE IS NO SEPARATION BETWEEN CREATOR AND CREATION. Instead of believing that the Universe was created by an outside force, or by a God, Wiccans believe that Deity exists within the physical world as awareness, consciousness, and self-direction. Because Deity is present in all things, we see creation as a process—the Universe is continually dying and rebirthing itself. These cycles of renewal can be as big as the lives of the Universe or as small as a day in the life of the Earth. This internal direction, this consciousness, is beautiful and sacred.

2. ALL THINGS ARE CONNECTED TO ONE ANOTHER. Everything we do has an effect on the rest of the Universe, like ripples in a pool of water or vibrations on a spider web. Nobody's actions happen in a vacuum or can be "taken back." It stands to reason that Witches would generally be environmentalists, but it's more than that. We have an individual responsibility to be aware of the way we affect

each other and the planet—not just physically, but emotionally, spiritually, and magically as well. The effect we have can and should be consciously directed to bring about a positive influence on the world around us.

3. SEXUALITY IS SACRED AND OUR BODIES ARE SACRED. We are sexual beings from birth. Between consenting adults, sexual union is a gift from the Gods. It is also a way of expressing the creative force between the dual aspects of Deity, the God and Goddess—even when you're alone or with someone of the same sex. Sexuality is one of the greatest mysteries of the Universe, for it has the ultimate potential to create life. When we experience our sexuality in a positive, life-affirming way, we are all creators, and so come closer to the Divine. Some Wiccans do their rituals skyclad (naked), mainly because they want to appear before the Gods as they were made, with no false personas. Pagans are, in general, more comfortable than most about being nude.

BLAIR: "I'm probably one of the few people that will admit they try to practice skyclad if at all possible. And it's not because of being really flaunty. I think clothing is something we weren't born with—I have never seen someone come out of the womb wearing a three-piece suit, or even a loincloth."

4. RELIGIOUS INSPIRATION COMES FROM NATURE. Before there were holy books, the earliest peoples looked to the physical world around them for clues to the meaning of life and death. They saw that everything moves in cycles: the moon, the Earth's seasons, day and night. The tree will sprout, grow, die, and fertilize the soil so that another tree may sprout in that place. Destruction and death are not bad or evil; they pave the way for new life. Human life happens in a cycle as well. We are born, we grow, we die, and we return again in another form. Not all Witches believe in reincarnation per se, but most will agree with the general principle. Because energy is never lost or gained, and matter cannot be destroyed, death is not an end, but a change. We do not believe in human life as a one-way passage that lands the person in heaven or hell for all eternity. Nothing else in Nature happens in a straight line; why should that?

5. WE HAVE AN INTIMATE AND PERSONAL CONNECTION WITH DEITY. The basic life-force, in its purest form, is hard to comprehend. In order to gain a more intimate connection, Wiccans connect to that force through various Deities that are physical, emotional, and embodied in basic life experiences. This way, rather than having to go secondhand through clergy or a holy book, we can experience Deity as being present and immediate. These Gods are seen by most Wiccans as essences of being—not actual omnipotent beings living up on a mountain. They are expressions of life: love, forgiveness, anger, celebration, sorrow. The Gods are real because we experience them firsthand, in everything we do.

We see the Gods as both male and female, because both are equally important in the creation of life. But because the life-force is infinite, the Gods have an infinite number of guises. The energy of Deity comes through us and through everything else in the world: humans, animals, plants, and earth alike. We limit the Gods by necessity—we define and personify them in order to get closer to Divinity; but one of the greatest Mysteries is that the life-force actually transcends all definitions.

6. EACH WICCAN IS CONSIDERED TO BE CLERGY. Each of us has the same ability to connect with Deity. Of course, someone who has studied the Craft for ten years will naturally be more adept at magic and ritual than someone who is brand-new; but the connection with Deity has nothing to do with the trappings of ritual—and therefore does not necessarily improve with time. It is intuitive and natural. If anything, learning more about the mechanics may bring someone further away from that simple understanding. When everyone is clergy, everyone is equally powerful—and that's an important political statement as well as a spiritual one.

7. MAGIC IS REAL, MAGIC WORKS, AND EVERYONE HAS THE ABILITY TO USE IT. Magic is sometimes defined as "the art of bringing change in accordance with will," in other words, channeling and directing the force of your own will to cause things to happen. There are lots of different theories as to how and why magic works, and these vary among cultures. In Witchcraft, the nature of the magic we do is interwoven with our beliefs about the world. All things and beings are connected by a web of energy. By using concen-

tration, props (like candles, incense, and such), symbols, or sounds, it is possible to affect this energy and bring change. This is an ability we are all born with, although it's not acknowledged, much less encouraged, in our society. Some have ignored it for so many years that, like a muscle that doesn't get used, their natural magical ability can seem almost dead. Still, a lot of us cast spells without even realizing it. Sometimes our emotions get out of hand and trigger our force of will: for instance, when you hurl a lot of anger at someone, he might start to feel sick. Or consider those times when an outpouring of love can heal emotional wounds.

8. WHAT GOES AROUND, COMES AROUND.   We might make our own distinctions between "black" and "white" magic, but in Nature, there is no concept of good or evil. Such absolutes require a judge, and the Gods do not judge, they simply are. The law of Nature is that of cause and effect. Because we are all so closely connected, we cannot harm one another without harming ourselves. And because of the extent to which a person must immerse himself in any spell he casts, all spells, for help or harm, will come back magnified. Hopefully, just having an understanding of this connection and the consequences of negativity should lead us to act responsibly. Of course, this isn't foolproof, but punishment is usually swift and appropriate.

Witchcraft is more than just a religion or a set of philosophies. It is a way of life, a way of existing within the Universe. It comes from ancient sources, but can change with the times; it is very serious in nature, but can laugh at itself. I could not possibly fit all that I could tell you about Witchcraft into an introduction, which is why I wrote the rest of this book. And all that you can learn about Witchcraft cannot be contained in a book, and will take at *least* a lifetime to learn.

When I was sixteen, I became a Witch. I wasn't sure of what I was doing, or even why I was doing it, but I was sure of one thing: that it was exactly what I wanted to be doing. That is the experience of the beginning seeker, and it is for that person that this book was created. Learn, practice, experiment, question, celebrate, and enjoy!

About the Exercises

Throughout the book you will find illustrative, constructive, and illuminating exercises to help guide your individual path. Here are guidelines to follow when doing these exercises, and when performing your own rituals. You know best what works best for you, so if you try it the way suggested here and you don't like it, go ahead and change it. Just make sure you change it for a reason. Try to do most of the exercises, especially those you feel unsure about. You may be pleasantly surprised! None of these involve a great amount of risk, so don't worry about that.

Find a space where you will not be disturbed. This is especially important if you are doing anything that requires any level of trance. It is disturbing and even harmful to be startled when you are meditating or otherwise "elsewhere." If you live with others, just close the door to your bedroom or put a sign on it. It's generally not a good idea to do the exercises in a public place, even in a beautiful park where you feel safe and comfortable. At best, there is a big risk of distractions, and at worst, if you are in a deep trance state, you may be vulnerable to physical attack. If your room is not respected as private space, just wait until all other members of the household have gone to bed, or go over to a friend's house. Make sure the area is as quiet as possible.

It *is* possible to do magic and ritual with distractions—an elder of mine once led a very effective ritual on a traffic island, on 42nd Street, in New York City—but it's tricky, and you don't need the hassle. To muffle those noises you can't control, you can play a tape of the ocean or a stream to mask the sound. Soft music is nice, but you might want to stick to natural sounds in the very beginning. They're more neutral and won't affect your mood as much.

Make sure you are physically comfortable. If the setting is private enough, you might want to take your clothes off. Otherwise, put on something light and nonconstricting. I include jeans in this; casual as they are, the waistband can really cut off your energy flow when you sit or bend over. Make sure you are not too warm or too cold, and that the light in the room is the way you like it. Also, don't do the exercises if you are very full or very hungry.

Get into an effective position.   If you are doing a relaxation exercise or a very involved trance, it can be tempting to lie down on your back, or even to get in bed. This is not usually a good idea, because most of us associate that position with sleep, and you may accidentally drift off during the exercise. This is not dangerous, but it's not effective either. The best position is to sit in a firm but comfortable chair, with your back straight, feet flat on the floor, and your hands resting on your thighs. Of course, some of the exercises will call for different positions, but this is the basic one. Sitting cross-legged is okay, or if you can get into a lotus position, go for it! (I sure as hell can't.)

Don't forget your mood.   If you are feeling anxious or very wound up, you should do the relaxation and grounding and centering exercises (given in the chapter on energy work) before attempting any of the others. It will help to calm you down and focus you. If you are very sleepy, depressed, or feeling physically ill, it's probably a good idea to wait till a better time. Beware of chronic procrastination, however!

Create an ambience.   One of the great things about Wicca is that we get to construct our own "churches," wherever we are. Your surroundings can have a very strong effect on you. Have you ever noticed that you can't seem to focus your mind if your desk is a mess? Or that you tend to relax when you dim the lights? Well, the first part of ritual is about changing your setting to influence your mind. Candles, robes, and beautiful statues of the Gods aren't just decorative, they also have a psychological effect. Try changing your setting in a way that helps you to get to the right state of mind. While keeping comfort a priority, sometimes it can make the exercise more powerful and meaningful if you also wear something that makes you feel like aqqqqqqqqqqq magical being. You can make a magical robe by tracing a big T-shirt shape on a piece of doubled-over fabric, and sewing around the edges. Light a candle, put on some inspiring music, open the windows to let the night air in, whatever you like. If the exercise or ritual you're doing doesn't work for you, it doesn't work, period!

Keep a journal. A "Book of Shadows" is the traditional Wiccan name for a magical journal. This can include, for instance, a record of spells and their outcomes, seasonal and rite-of-passage rituals, herbal formulas, astrological information, meditations, poems, and songs. Sometimes a Book of Shadows is passed down from coven to coven in its original form and is only available to those initiated into that tradition (Gerald Gardner's Book of Shadows is one example). As a solitary, your journal will be just for your use, so you can do anything you want with it. You should write down the outcomes of the exercises you do and any rituals you perform. Your journal should fulfill a dual purpose:

1. It will be a place for you to keep useful information handy for reference (such as the names and dates of the sabbats, the eight seasonal festivals).
2. It will be someplace for you to record your opinions, feelings, and intuitions about the Craft.

Together, these elements will provide a record of your magical growth. There are no rules about what to include. Throw in a couple of jokes if you want! Your journal can and should change and expand over time. And who knows, maybe someday your students will be passing it down to their initiates, just like Gerald Gardner's journal!

CHAPTER TWO

Energy Work and the Elements

Energy Work: The Root of Magic

MISHA: "The magic that I do is all involved with healing energy. When I do bodywork on friends and people I care about, I seem to be able to release energy blockages, and in that release I tend to feel the emotions that were involved in the blockages. Some people have had horrible experiences in their lives, and those are part and parcel of the trauma left in their bodies. It's a wonderful and rather horrible experience to feel that pass through you as you release it, through pressure, through touch. . . . And the thing I love about it is it's the ultimate in moral magic, because the worst thing you can do is nothing. . . . With touches and energy so relatively gentle, causing harm would be impossible."

Pagans have known for centuries that when they worship and honor Nature, they are honoring the spirit of life itself, which dwells within the physical world. Pagans commonly refer to that spirit as "energy," though it shouldn't be confused with the scientific term. (There may be parallels between the two, but since I'm not a physicist, I'm just going to discuss the kind of energy we work with when we do magic.)

Magical energy can be called "magical" or "psychic" energy, sometimes "power," even "the force," depending on your point of reference. It's all the same thing. In some Asian religions and in martial arts, it's called *chi*. To Pagans, that force is a tool to use in magic, and it is the sacred Consciousness, the nameless, faceless presence of the Divine.

In order to do effective magic, it is essential to understand the nature of energy, how it works, and how to work with it. An intuitive understanding of energy will bring you closer to the Gods. Energy work is the core of all Wiccan practice.

In magical thinking, Deity is constantly manifesting and re-creating the world we see, and it does so from within. Each of us is connected to that power, and we can use it to do magical work. However, life energy as a whole is greater than any of us. When you do energy work, remember to keep the balance between your needs and wants, and the natural flow of the Universe.

It is unfortunate that the dominant image of Witchcraft in our society evokes "bending forces to your will." In that kind of practice, magical energy is treated like electricity: an unlimited supply of power that can be used to achieve what we want. It's easy to see why some Pagans and Wiccans get into a "power trip."

But magical energy is not a neutral force. The Universe is *conscious*. Our personal energy, that which we can raise or lower, and that which we use to do magic and ritual—that energy is sacred, a direct link to the Divine. We must stay mindful of the larger picture, the well of life from which our power springs. It is wrong to use that energy for selfish or harmful reasons. Yes, we have power and we have free will, but we do not operate in a vacuum. We must use our power responsibly. The chapter on magic goes into magical ethics in more depth.

Before you start learning how to manipulate and move psychic energy outside yourself—that is, to work magic or do healing—you will need to learn how to sense and control your personal energy. You will notice that some days you have an endless supply.

You bounce around, cheerful and productive. Other days all you want to do is sleep. These energy shifts can be traced to your psychic self, the body of energy that exists both within your physical form and extends for a few feet outside of it. It is also sometimes called the "aura." Your psychic energy can both affect, and be affected by, your physical, mental, and emotional selves. Therefore, it is essential to learn how to nurture and maintain it.

✂ EXERCISE: Sensing Your Psychic Energy

Hold your hands up about an inch apart, palms facing each other. You might feel a tingling, cold, heat, or a breeze brush over your palms. If it seems weak or if you don't feel anything at all, you can turn up the power simply by willing it so. Take a deep breath, imagine yourself drawing energy up from the ground, up through your body, and pouring it out through your palms. See the energy coming together in the center, between your palms, into a little dense cloud or sphere. Hold it for a minute or so. Then be sure to reabsorb it into your palms, or you might accidentally drain yourself. If the energy gets to be too much, touch your palms to the floor or ground for a few seconds and see the energy sinking down. If this exercise doesn't work for you, it doesn't necessarily mean that your energy is low; you might just need to get more in touch with your will. If you are feeling low (hungry, tired, or depressed), try it another time when you're feeling more "up."

The following two exercises are probably the most important in the book. When you know how to relax, ground, and center yourself effectively, you will be able to handle almost any situation the Universe can throw your way. These exercises are especially important to do before any kind of work in which there is conscious movement of energy—meditation, spellwork, ritual, divination, and so forth. And remember, there are also times when you are unconsciously moving psychic energy. Relaxing, grounding and centering can be extremely helpful at those times too: confrontations with people, making love, falling asleep, exercising, and creating art or music. Together with regular exercise, I believe they are a cure for stress.

Before you start, get as comfortable as possible. This means that ideally you should wear nonconstricting clothing (or no clothing at all), you should have dim lighting, a comfortably warm room, a good chair that enables you to sit upright with your back supported, and either soft music or silence. (Of course, if you are doing this technique on the subway, driving in your car, or at work, do the best you can. Magic is meant to be done in the real world, and conditions are not always ideal.) No matter the restrictions, relaxing, grounding, and centering will be good for you.

 EXERCISE: Relaxation

First, become aware of your breathing. Do not force your breath; let it come in and go out. Your body knows how to do this; you don't have to help. Just bring your attention to it. Simply doing this can be very grounding by itself; it's a good trick to know, for when you don't have much time. Don't dwell on any thoughts; let them come and go as easily as your breath. Trying to think about nothing just doesn't work. It's better to let your mind drift, and if a thought comes up, return your awareness to your breathing. It will go away. Do this for a couple of minutes, as long as feels right.

Now focus your attention on your toes, continuing to breathe easily. Give them permission to relax. Think them heavy, think them limp. If this sounds silly, remember about one part affecting the whole. Even just consciously relaxing one part of your body will begin to relax the rest.

After your toes are completely relaxed (and it may take longer than you think—don't rush it), move to the balls of your feet. Progress up your entire body, noticing the tension that's already there in each part, and allowing each one to let the tension go. Of course, "forcing" yourself to relax just will not work. Tension is the unnatural state; relaxation is natural. Once you let the tension go, you will be relaxed.

As you move up your body, don't forget the buttocks (those contain large muscles that can hold a lot of tension), your stomach muscles, and your face and head. Once you get to the top of your head, scan your whole body mentally and gently relax any part that still carries tension.

Finally, return your awareness to your breathing for a few minutes, to regain a sense of stillness and serenity.

✤ EXERCISE: Grounding and Centering

This technique reestablishes your connection with the earth, both through movement of energy and also through the conscious decision to become mentally and emotionally aware of that connection.

First, relax. Either do the entire relaxation exercise, or a shortened version.

Now imagine that, like a tree, you have roots that you can push down into the ground, from wherever you are touching the floor or chair (from your feet, your back, or your buttocks). It doesn't matter if you are actually sitting on the ground, or on a floor, or in an airplane. With energy, physical location is irrelevant. This is where visualization is very important; to see something in a way that isn't dependent on the physical, to see a different level of reality. We are always connected to the earth on the most basic level, no matter where we are.

As you exhale, push your roots down. As you inhale, pull up energy from the earth. You might want to breathe a little deeper now, just to emphasize what you're doing. (Don't hyperventilate, for goodness' sake!) Breathe from low in your body, from your belly. You can imagine your roots going through the floor, the concrete of the foundation of the building, the topsoil, the hard ground, the cool dark earth, the bedrock, and so forth. Or you can just skip all that and visualize the earth right under you. You are extending your own personal psychic energy down into Mother Earth, to reestablish your connection with her.

The exercise is over when you have extended your energy down as far as you feel you need to go to feel truly rooted, and when the energy you pull up from the earth is filling your whole body. Then there will be no separation between your personal energy and that of the earth below you. You will reach a state of balance, and you will be grounded and centered. You determine for yourself when you have reached that point.

The way you will feel afterward depends on the state you were in when you started. If you were unbalanced in any way beforehand, you will notice a swing in the other direction. If you were tense at the beginning, now you will feel especially relaxed. If you were tired, sleepy, and in need of energy, then you'll feel invigorated. Whatever you need, the earth will restore it to you. And now you are ready to do energy work.

Always ground and center before doing any magical work.

What will happen if you do not ground and center before doing energy work? I found out the hard way, once. During a beautiful summer thunderstorm, my college friends and I decided to do a spontaneous power-raising out in front of our dorm. I led everyone through the grounding and centering exercise, but didn't think to do it along with them. We danced, chanted, raised the power, and sent it off. Then my knees buckled. I was almost completely drained. I had to be practically carried back to my room. Magical mishaps aren't always quite so dramatic, but it's better not to take chances. When your energy is steady and balanced, you have some degree of insurance.

In order to see psychic energy, all you need to do is tune your eyes to the right frequency. The physical world will go slightly out of focus, and you will be able to see the beautiful waves and colors of the energy all around us. It's not nearly as difficult to see the human energy field, or aura, as it might seem at first. When you watch a movie, you'll notice that the focus of the camera can change between something close and something far away. You know that you can make things go blurry by refocusing your eyes in a certain way. If you like to look at stereograms, like those in the "Magic Eye" books, you've already a seasoned pro with the nessesary technique.

❧ EXERCISE: Seeing the Aura

Have a friend stand in front of a blank white wall. It's easiest to do this exercise with another person, but if you're alone, you can use your hand instead. The human aura is usually brightest right above the head. Make sure you have enough light in the room. When you get better at this, you'll be able to do it with your eyes closed.

Stand across the room from your friend, or if you're using your own hand, put your arm out as far as it will stretch, and make sure that it has simple blank white wall as a background.

Now, relax. Don't squint or otherwise strain to see anything. (That is a surefire way of failing.) Simply let yourself gaze at the space right above the top of your friend's head, or right off the tips of your fingers. Don't work at it; let it come to you. You will probably see a slight white glow fairly soon. Keep looking, and expand your focus to a few inches away from the skin. Remember not to *try* to look at it. When you strain to see something, you are using the focus meant for the physical world, and it will make the energy field disappear. Gaze at the space as if you were daydreaming in history class. Soon you will start to see that the glow extends farther out, and you will start to see colors. The human aura actually extends a few feet from the body, but most people can't see it past six inches or so. (It can be *sensed* further away, though—hence the idea of "personal space.")

Now have your friend try to consciously puff out his aura (or send energy out from the tips of your fingers). It will, of course, help if the person in question has done some energy work before. But if not, he can just visualize it, and you should see the light grow or become brighter.

If you stand in front of opposite walls, you can have a contest to see who can make her aura brighter. (Do the grounding and centering exercise first, just to help ensure you don't get burnt out.) Try to project certain colors. Of course, you can do all these things on your own, projecting your energy out from your fingers.

In the beginning you won't be able to see that much of the aura; perhaps just a few inches. With practice, you will be able to see more. There is no definite line where one person's aura stops and the energy of the room or the person next to him begins. Just like the light from a candle, it continues infinitely, even though you won't be able to see it after a point. The energy fields of all things are interwoven.

Now you know something about psychic energy. You know how to ground and center. From the exercise with your hands, and from doing the aura work, you know a bit about moving that energy around.

The next step is to work with your own energy to make sure you always have enough, and to make sure your psychic and physical bodies stay healthy and unblocked. After that, you can start to do energy work affecting others. If your own energy is unhealthy, you cannot perform an effective hands-on healing of another person, no matter how good your intentions. You can't do good work with damaged tools.

When you are working with psychic energy, you are deliberately bypassing the physical plane and going straight to the metaphysical, where it is much easier to affect others. This is why magic works, and this is also why you must be careful.

If you're just in a bad mood, that can have a negative emotional effect on the people around you. But if your energy is low, the damage can be much worse. Many people unconsciously drain energy off others, which can be very damaging. To prevent yourself from inadvertently becoming an "energy vampire," you must maintain your energy at a high enough level, and you must maintain an effective energy shield.

Taking Care of Your Own Psychic Energy

First, you will need to notice when your energy is low. You may feel tired, irritable, depressed, nervous, distracted, or dizzy. You may find yourself becoming emotionally clingy. You may feel that you need *something*, but not know what it is. Or you may have a totally different signal, unique to you, that indicates your energy has dropped. I usually get the munchies, and even when I've eaten as much as I can, I still somehow feel hungry.

There are many ways to raise the level of your psychic energy. Some of them are destructive things we do unconsciously: eating compulsively, smoking, having casual sex, and even provoking fights. But there are other methods just as effective, that are a lot better for you. Here are a few of them:

Make sure you are getting enough rest, and enough food and water. Drinking the oft-prescribed eight glasses of water a day can help to keep your energy clear and clean.

Take care of yourself emotionally. Do things that you find nurturing, whether that means putting on some favorite music, going out to a movie, or curling up with a trashy novel. Try to cultivate healthy relationships with other people, and try not to allow those in your life to leave you frazzled.

Your mental health is also important. Hours spent in front of the TV will cause your energy to plummet. You may have noticed the dazed feeling you have when you've spent a day on the couch. Get regular mental stimulation; you can feed off that. Every time I learn something I feel my energy rise.

Finally, sometimes the quickest way to replenish your psychic energy is to do something you find spiritually uplifting. Light a candle, spend some time in quiet meditation, do the grounding and centering exercise, sit under a tree and smell the grass.

Because all the aspects of your person—physical, mental, emotional, and spiritual—are interconnected, anything you do to replenish your energy in one area will help your whole self. To be more precise, however, if you notice your energy is low, think about where the problem is. Are you physically tired? Do something that will bring your physical energy back, such as taking a nap or going for a walk in the fresh air. If you're feeling depressed, rent a silly movie.

These days, many people don't take good care of themselves. We can choose whether we want to sit and wait for the Gods to "fix it,"—which will be a long wait—or we can heal ourselves. According to magical thinking, we are each responsible for our own energy and our own well-being. As Witches, it is one of our jobs to work positive magic, to improve the world in which we live. That must start with healing and nurturing ourselves.

Shielding

JAKE: "When you walk into a room and you feel unsafe, or you're walking outside and feel unsafe, shielding means putting up a protective barrier or an invisible sign over your head. It's like a combination of a cloaking device and a 'don't mess with me' kind of thing. I noticed this especially walking around my old college at night. I have always found that when I have this protective shield/cloaking device up, I never feel threatened, and the people I pass, I know that they won't mess with me. And coincidentally, the one day I was walking and didn't have it up, I was actually confronted."

Part of magical responsibility means maintaining an energy shield, which serves much the same function as the energy circle cast before doing most magic and ritual: It keeps unwanted influences from coming in, and it keeps your personal energy from leaking out. It's not like a brick wall; you don't want to be cut off from the rest of the world, but you need protection from psychic static, and you'll need to protect others from your own energy fluctuations. It's sort of like using sunblock at the beach. It's a filter—a necessary protection.

Putting up a shield is a simple matter of visualization, or imagination. One of the first steps toward magical thinking is the belief in the power of your mind and your intent. Choose an image for your shield and see it there. Know it is there, beyond a shadow of a doubt. If you feel it start to fade, see it coming back. You will not need to strain or push. If you are doing it right, you will have a sense of quiet certainty.

The image you choose for your shield should depend on what you need at the time. Most of the time I imagine simple clear glass. Almost invisible, but a barrier nonetheless. Just enough to give me a sense of my own space. But sometimes, if I'm feeling threatened, I will put up something more opaque, such as the branches of a tree. If I need to feel nurtured and comfortable, then it's a soft blue blanket. Someday you may find yourself in a situation that calls for barbed wire. Use whatever you feel you need, just keep in mind that it can often be sensed by others. It is part of the image you project. You cannot be shielded with a deathly force field and then try to transmit a loving, nurturing feeling to someone else. It won't work. Whatever shield you use, try to make sure you always have one. Ours is an unpredictable world, and you deserve some protection.

Learning to take care of your own psychic energy can be very difficult. I spent years studying the Craft. I learned about mythology, magical philosophy, the structure of ritual, and divination.

But all that was useless when I found myself being drained of energy over and over again. I still often forget to maintain it. The lesson I am continually learning is that positive magic and worship are meaningless without self-love and self-nurturance. Take care of yourself, and most of the rest will follow naturally.

Too often I have seen people take energy work for granted. That's ironic, because an understanding and awareness of your own energy and that of your environment is essential for you to be able to take proper care of yourself and work effective magic. Don't dismiss it as esoteric knowledge; it's not.

The Elements

Air, fire, water, and earth: These are the four basic elements used in many disciplines, from astrology to Oriental medicine. Within all Wiccan traditions, these four essences make up the physical and nonphysical Universe.

If you remain mindful of the forces of the four elements in your life—in any way you feel them—you will become more aware of your surroundings and more in control of your own energy. The system of the five elements (the fifth being spirit) is just that: a system. It's a way of defining the world. It helps us to keep a balance in our lives, and it helps us to call on a particular part of ourselves when we need it. That's not to say the elements aren't real. They are as real as you choose to make them. I will outline below their meaning in Wiccan magic and ritual.

Air

Associated with the east and the rising sun. Represents thought, intellectual processes, intuitive and psychic work. Wind. The breath of the body. The sense of smell. Animals: anything that flies; birds, insects. The *athame* (dagger) is the tool of air.

Fire

Associated with the south and the noonday sun. Represents passion and will, purification, transformation, sexuality. The sun.

The heat of the body. The sense of sight. Animals: lions, dragons, phoenix. The *wand* is the tool of fire.

Water

Associated with the west and the setting sun. Represents emotion and intuition, love and sorrow. The ocean. The womb and blood. The sense of taste. Animals: anything that swims; fish, dolphins, and whales. The *chalice* is the tool of water.

Earth

Associated with the north and midnight. Represents the physical world, stability, practicality, silence. The mountains. The bones of the body, the sense of touch. Animals: anything solid or earth-dwelling; bulls, the stag, worms, moles. The *pentacle* (disk, stone) is the tool of earth.

Spirit/Center/Akasha

This isn't an element like the others; rather, it's the life energy that extends through and joins all of them. It is associated with the center of the circle, and eternity. It represents transcendence and immanence, the void, the presence of Deity, the spirit of the body, the sense of hearing or intuition. The *cauldron* is the tool of spirit.

Each of us contains all of the elements in varying amounts, depending on the nature of our personalities. If you are a very intellectual person, you have an affinity toward the element of air. If you are very emotional, that's water. Each of us also has elements with which we are uncomfortable. For instance, you may be afraid of anger or sexuality (fire), or you may have trouble dealing with emotional turmoil (water). Many Pagans, when asked to call on an element for a ritual, call one that they already feel close to. This is counterproductive in the search for balance. Elements that are problematic for you are the ones you should meditate upon, work with, and bring into your life—not the ones you already "like."

✦ EXERCISE: Make Yourself Uncomfortable!

Pick one of the four elements that bothers you, upsets you, bores you, frightens you, makes you feel sick—whichever one you like the least. Relax, ground, center, and set up sacred space (see chapter 6 on ritual). Remind yourself that you are in a safe place. Take a deep breath and let yourself sink into a meditative state. Now, call on that element. Use any imagery that you strongly associate with it. Throw yourself right in. Imagine diving into the ocean, hang-gliding, running through an inferno, covering your body with dirt. Why does it bother you? Why have you been avoiding it? What do you need from that element that you haven't been getting? What do you need to do, to bring it into your life and balance yourself? When you feel you've gotten your answers, come back to everyday consciousness. Write about this in your journal. Don't forget to follow up on it; imbalances won't be corrected in one sitting.

In the course of one's life, there will be times when it is appropriate to be more deeply involved with one element than another. When you're falling in love, you'll be immersed in a lot of fire and water, and not much else. Your job may demand that you be in touch with the intellectual quality of air. But these states are not absolutes. For instance, air, cool and detached as it is, is out of place in a romantic relationship—unless it requires a clearer perspective. The passionate energy of fire could be trouble at work, unless, say, you need help getting psyched up for a sales presentation.

Generally speaking, the idea is to work with opposites for balance. If your work situation is very fiery and stressful, try aligning yourself with water. You can sit at your desk and imagine yourself floating in a mountain lake for a few minutes, or, later on that night, you might go construct an elaborate ritual with all sorts of water symbols, water Deities, and appropriate colors and music.

There are also times when one or another of the elements will make itself known in a manner that is difficult to ignore.

BLAIR: "During the Beltane ritual one year, we decided it would be a neat idea to put candles into the swimming pool, to have them float around. Well, we went away, had circle, then someone yelled, 'The pool's on fire!' The candles had floated to the side and set the liner on fire. The next year, they decided to take a nice glass-lined bowl; they put burning oil into it and lit it. And as everyone was looking into it, it shattered, and splattered oil everywhere. The year after that, one of the candles fell over and somehow heated up a glass globe that exploded. That takes us up to this year, and we don't want to know what's going to happen this year!"

When I told this story to my partner, I remarked that perhaps Blair's group should try working with a different kind of imagery. He replied ironically, "Yeah, watch, they start working with water and wind up drowning." It's unclear whether the fire imagery is the problem, the group's chemistry isn't right, or they just need to ground their energy more effectively. Either way, the constant "bonfires" should be a wake-up call to pay some more attention to what's really going on. I'm not one to find omens in everything, but it's hard to call all of this coincidence.

When all four elements are balanced and connected through spirit, an individual is healthy on all levels. In Wiccan ritual, when someone invokes, calls, or aligns himself with the four elements, he is balancing his own energy, as well as that of the circle he is inside.

Just like magical energy in general, the elements exist both within and outside of us. We have a lot of control over them, but we also need to live in balance with our environment. It is always better to work from the inside out. It's important to understand what you are doing when you call on the elements. You are not actually saying, "Hey, come over here," to some astral being on the other side of the Veil. The four elements are names we give to *qualities* of being. So when you call on the power, the force of the element earth, you are bringing solidity out of yourself. You are recognizing stability in the world around you. You are becoming a mountain of stone, unmovable and unshakable. You are changing your consciousness to change your own energy and the energy of any circles you are working within.

It's possible to find lists of correspondences for the elements (and for other things, like the sun and moon) in many magical books. Starhawk's *Spiral Dance* has some excellent ones that I used as inspiration here. These lists are meant to be a jumping-off point. You will develop your own associations, and some of them will probably differ from these. Maybe you'll decide that, for you, fire represents emotional love and water is about transformation. Maybe the associations will change depending on your situation. It's personal, and it's fluid.

Magic is about manifesting your will. Call up the elements and join with them!

CHAPTER THREE

Deity

VICTORIA: "If I could be with any of the Gods, I'd really like to hang out with Lugh. The story goes that as a mortal, he went to see a king to get entrance to his kingdom, and was asked, 'What do you have to offer?' He said, 'I'm a metalsmith,' and they said, 'We have one of those.' He said, 'I'm a bard,' and they said, 'Got one.' He listed like fifty billion different things, and finally he said, 'Well, do you have a man who can do all of that?' For me, it validated being a multifaceted person."

Wicca isn't just about the mechanisms of magic. The presence and reality of the Gods is central to the practice of the Craft. They guide, they love, they influence our lives in countless ways. Without some idea of a universal consciousness, we would be doing our magic in a bleak world of mechanical cause and effect, with no inspiration or goal for our magical work. The idea of Deity takes our practice to a deeper level of reality. The Gods are present, right here, right now, and they are waiting for us to discover them.

DAVID: "When I see the Pagan Gods, I do not see the vengeful, jealous omnipotence of the Christian Deity. My Gods have a sense of humor; when I screw up, they laugh at my silly human foolishness. When I cry, they cry with me, and dry my tears with their love. When I drain my bottle of mead amidst the swirling bodies and dancing flames of a drumming circle, they smile contentedly at my enjoyment of the gift of life—and then send the headache the next morning, just to make sure that I remember that all things have a price!"

The Wiccan View of Deity

Most of us were led to believe that God is male, separate from the world, lives up in heaven, watches and controls everything that happens on Earth, and judges us according to how we live.

That's why people say, "Oh, do you worship trees?" when they hear ours is a Nature religion. To them, we are actually praying to, and celebrating, one insignificant ball of dirt somewhere on an outer arm of the Milky Way galaxy. But in the Craft, the physical Universe is not dead. It is an outward manifestation of the Divine. My dictionary defines *nature* first as "the essential character of a thing; quality or qualities that make something what it is; essence." We are *essence* worshippers!

There is no parent-God in charge. The Universe—by which I mean all beings and all matter—has its own internal consciousness and direction. There's no one "up there" to tell us what to do or punish us if we do something wrong. We are all equally responsible and powerful, as embodiments of the Divine. Although humans are not special as far as our connection to Deity, our role is more challenging. You see, animals seem to be intuitively conscious of that connection, while we humans tend to forget it all the time.

In Wicca and Neo-Paganism, a common phrase is "Thou art God," taken from Robert Heinlein's *Stranger in a Strange Land*. It isn't intended to fluff up one's ego; it simply means we should remember our Divine Source, remember the God that dwells within. It will take a while before you can really take in that understanding, particularly if you've got a rotten self-image or are feeling powerless. That sort of realization—what we call a Mystery—can only come with time, and it usually comes as a surprise.

Who Are the Wiccan Gods?

> MARGOT: "It's not about worship, it's about respect. It's about learning, about exploring. When people hear the word *worship,* they see someone going down on bended knee with head and eyes lowered, in a position of, if nothing else, some kind of minor spiritual inferiority. My journey has been about keeping my back straight and my eyes open, and giving respect where respect is due."

Although Wiccans recognize Deity as a universal force, we tend to concentrate on different aspects of that force. This is for two reasons: First of all, we look to Nature for our spiritual inspiration, and Nature is hugely diverse. Second, many of us find the "genderless and infinite" idea of God much too vague to grab onto. We need something more personal!

In this way, Wicca can be considered both monotheistic and polytheistic. The different Deities are facets of one diamond. When we say "the Gods," we don't mean a literal group of superheroes. We are speaking of the universal life-force in all its many forms.

> OBSIDIANA: "It's nice to have these little pictures of pretty people, and say 'that's this one, and that's that one.' Maybe it sparks the imagination, so you can imagine the personality type that is trying to be described. But any Deities I've worked with, regardless of pantheon, are not people. They're energies, and people give names to these energies. When you think about it, we as people are just energy inside a body, and it's really not that different."

Because of this belief, any pantheon (system of Deities) can be incorporated into Wicca. People may work within Hindu, Greek, Hebrew, Norse, Native American, Celtic, or Roman pantheons. Mixing Deities from different groups in the same ritual is usually frowned upon—it gets confusing—but aside from that, there's a lot of room to experiment. In the Wiccan belief, all images of the Divine are equally valid.

The current mainstream image of God—an old bearded white guy in the sky—is actually a relatively new one. One of the earliest known works of art is the now-famous *Venus of Willendorf,* a statue dating back to 30,000 B.C.E., found in Austria—of a pregnant woman with huge breasts, which is believed to represent the Earth Goddess. If you had to choose a gender for the Deity of creation, it would have be female. Women give birth, women nurse children. Fertility Goddesses can be found in almost all cultures—from the Greek Gaia to the Virgin Mary, so complete unto herself, and so close to the Source that she needed no human father to bear her child.

It's important to note that the word *fertility* does not just refer to the ability to make babies. The first definition in my dictionary is "producing abundantly, fruitful," before any mention of giving birth. To ancient peoples, the Goddess would bring not only children but good crops, wealth, and contentment. To us, fertility can mean happiness, money, success in our career, friends, good food, and a nice home. When we say that we practice a fertility religion, it means we celebrate the bounty of the Earth as well as creativity: the ability to bring something new into the world. This *can* refer to a child, but any project or undertaking can be your "baby"!

Still, it takes both men and women to create life. The Goddess alone is incomplete. Archeologists have also found a French cave painting dating back to the same time period, which depicted a male figure with horns, or antlers, on his head. This is believed by some to represent the Horned God of the hunt. Half man, half animal, he represents the connection between civilization and wilderness. Similar images can be found in different, later pantheons represented as, among others, Herne, Cernunnos, Pan, and even the Christian Devil.

The Horned God is a creature very different from the Earth Goddess. He is also a fertility figure, but this is *male* fertility. Where the Goddess is receptive, the God is aggressive. The phallus, the sword, the staff, the maypole, the winding vine—all these are symbols of the God. He is the activating, dynamic force in Nature.

The Sacred Marriage

The world as we know it is built upon polarity. The Earth passes through day and night. The sun and moon take turns ruling the sky. Warmth and cold fall over the Earth, one after the other. Without death, there would be no life. This is the way Deity shows itself to us, in the interplay between opposites. It isn't possible to separate the male from the female; they are intertwined forever.

That's why, in Wicca, we usually honor the Divine as God and Goddess (also called the Lord and Lady). Craft tradition teaches that "All Gods are one God, all Goddesses are one Goddess, and there is but one Initiator." All images of Deity are equally valid, and all are facets of the Goddess and God. The Goddess and God, when united, become the One, the Source, the Initiator.

Within Wicca, there are also some groups—mostly women— whose traditions place a stronger emphasis on the female force in Nature. The God, if mentioned, is incidental. This imbalance is supposedly a counterweight to hundreds of years of patriarchy, and it is seen as necessary before we can swing back to the middle. I can understand that reasoning, but I prefer to *remake* the idea of the male God into a loving, sensual, wild, and fun sort of Deity—rather than to trash the entire idea of maleness as sacred.

Within a balanced framework, however, it makes sense that some will devote their worship and work, for a time, to one par-ticular aspect of the Divine. For the past few years, for instance, I have leaned much more strongly to the male side of things and only lately have felt the need to connect with the Goddess.

BLAIR: "I am extremely Goddess-oriented, to the fact that's one of the main reasons I don't think I ever linked with other religions. Just because I don't see the Divine as being a male figurehead at all. If it's going to be one gender, it's going to be a woman, just because I have this strong thought of birth. I do believe in male and female, but also my sexual orientation that does influence me. I am biased. But I do give praise to both."

Most Witches, however, worship and honor the Lord and Lady equally as partners, lovers, and cocreators. They may call on the Gods by name; Ares and Aphrodite are one couple, Cernunnos and Aradia are another. Or they may call on them by the qualities they have: "Dark Lord" and "Bright Lady," or "God of the Greenwood" and "Goddess of the Fields." As my partner puts it, the God is the "All that is Male" and the Goddess the "All that is Female." We give them names and faces, but they are actually infinite.

That's why you are free to reject the traditional definitions if the Gods speak to you differently. The God and Goddess are complementary opposites. When we talk about them, we assign to them what one might call "traditional" masculine and feminine qualities. This is not to imply that the Goddess is always sweet and motherly, or that the God is always aggressive and lusty. There's no reason why the Goddess can't be a butch biker chick and the God a drag queen. There are thousands of different Gods and Goddesses in all the traditions around the world, and they're all valid. Even then, each of us will see a particular Deity in a slightly different way, and there are even more faces of God.

> OBSIDIANA: "The creative force behind the Universe is just beyond our comprehension. Even within monotheistic religions, there are as many different concepts of their "one God" as there are practitioners! And every one of them is valid, because if the force that created the universe encompasses everything, how can any aspect of it be wrong?"

✂ EXERCISE: Who Are *Your* Gods?

> Spend some time meditating on the God and the Goddess, each on a different day. What is the essence of male, or female to you? Are these something you've been taught, or more like a truth you *know*? Who does the Goddess herself tell you she is? Who do you know the God is? Is he a lover? A father? A dark and frightening Mystery? Is the Goddess an elusive fairy? A stately Earth Mother?

If the idea of "male" and "female" is too huge and complex for you (understandable), and you need to narrow the focus, read about and meditate on a particular God and Goddess that you feel drawn toward. If you don't know of any, go to the mythology section in your library.

Create sacred space and spend some time meditating on that image of Deity. Welcome it, greet it in love and joy. You could create an elaborate ritual, or just change your surroundings. For instance, meditate on the Crone on an autumn night with the windows open and the smell of leaves in the air. Greet the Horned God in a lush summer forest.

When you feel you have really joined with that Deity, draw a picture of what (or who) you experienced, write a song, a poem, or a story. You may object that you don't do "creative" things like that. But you need to use a different part of your psyche to understand and connect with the Gods. They cannot be accessed through logic.

So what's the point? This is one of the most important ideas in the Craft: Deity reveals itself in a different way, no less true, to each and every person. Our ability to visualize Deity is important, but our ability to bring it out is even more so. You must shift your focus, change your consciousness to become aware of those things you have forgotten or don't want to see. Why *can't* God be female? A serpent? A child? A mountain? And the more you open yourself to possibilities like these, the more fully you will be living a magical life.

✤ EXERCISE: Spend a Week With a God/dess

Read as much information as you can about a Deity that you find appealing. Then ask him or her to adopt you for a week, either silently and internally, or in the context of a formal ritual. You might do a daily devotional when you get up each morning. For the whole week, let your God/dess show you a few things. Watch for how that Deity manifests in your life. (Take care when you choose your Deity. I was under Kali's care for a few months, and it was scary—though I don't regret it at all) Remember that the Gods are not elsewhere; they show their faces all the time. At the end of the week, thank your God/dess, and spend some time writing or thinking about your experience.

Remember, though, that balance is important. At different times in your life, you will be drawn to different Deities or aspects of

Deities. As you learn about them, honor them, and work with them, stay mindful of their opposites and complements. Just as we should never celebrate spring without remembering winter, so we should never honor the bounty of the Earth Goddess Demeter without giving a nod to Hades, Lord of the cold and barren underworld. The danger of polytheism is that we can come to neglect the whole in regarding each of its parts separately. Remember the opposites, and remember that they are parts of the Whole.

The God and Goddess each manifest through both men and women. The Goddess tends to show her face more through women, and the God through men—but again, we must remember to strive for balance, both in our magical work and for the sake of our emotional well-being. Each of us should try to connect with the aspects of Deity that are most opposite to ourselves, in order not only to balance ourselves, but to reenact that most sacred of unions: that of light and dark, male and female, sun and moon.

Joining With the Gods

Union with the Divine is the goal of just about every religion. The Christians believe that Jesus greets us in death. Jewish mystics join with God through prayer and ritual. To Zen Buddhists, this union occurs the instant the idea of personal ego is released. In Wicca, all these are ways to the Gods—and there are more: drumming, dancing, chanting, ritual, magic, and the simple, "mundane" acts of love and kindness.

But to most (and maybe to you), all that stuff is mystical mumbo jumbo. There are three reasons most people never connect with the Divine. First, they may not believe in God at all. In our society, we are taught to believe only in those things which can be perceived through the five senses. And so our attention and energy is totally focused on the physical plane. If there's no "proof," why waste your time?

Second, if they do believe in God, the very way they think about him makes the experience impossible. Being alive in a material world precludes experiencing a God who lives separate and apart from that world. It's kind of like having a grandparent who lives in another state and never comes around to visit. If you can't walk beside him, how can you be *sure* he's really there?

Third, they leave such things up to the clergy and those folks considered "enlightened." The truth of God's existence must be taken at face value from the holy books and the clergy.

So if you want to experience the Divine, you must first change your perspective. You are already joined with the Divine right now, just by virtue of your existence. There is nothing that is separate from God/dess. When we join with the Gods, we are not going out to them, or drawing them in to us. We are really only shifting our consciousness to make ourselves aware of something that has been there all along. There is no need for an interpreter, no need for a book. Since we already carry within us the sparks of divinity, all we need do is look within and open ourselves to that awareness.

On the other hand, it does require a certain amount of "going further" to consciously connect with it, or in Pagan terms, "going *deeper*." The physical world we see and experience is sacred, and part of God/dess, but it is only the tip of the iceberg. Turning your sights to a more elemental kind of energy is what makes the difference between worshipping the physical world and worshipping the life-force within.

How do we become aware of that deep connection? There are many ways. The good news is you can start right now, and you will notice results immediately. The bad news is that the process, to be really lasting and permanent, can take a lifetime. Ever hear of "nirvana?" "self-actualization?" "serenity?" All these terms describe the feeling of living in union with the Divine.

The key is to forget these lies we have learned and repeated: that matter and spirit are disconnected; that God is limited to one face, one name, and one location; that objects, souls, and egos are separate and isolated from each other.

Some of the many ways to experience the Divine:

1. ALTER YOUR CONSCIOUSNESS. Move your viewpoint away from the surface world, so you can be aware of reality on a deeper level. This can be done through drumming, dancing, chanting, quiet meditation, exercise, sex, sleep, and yes, even some drugs—

though with all the legal and safe methods available, why take that risk?

2. SPEND TIME OUTDOORS. Certainly the wooden boards of your house are full of the Divine life-force, but it is much easier to be aware of that energy in the original trees. Go for a walk. Sit on your porch. Spend the day in a park. Camp out for a week. Experience the changes of the weather and the seasons, not as isolated scientific occurrences, but as the dance of life. Imagine different aspects of Nature as having personalities: the forest as a God, alive, laughing and covered in leaves; the ocean as a Goddess, huge and bountiful and mysterious. Don't bother trying to remember weird names from foreign pantheons, if it's not your thing; these experiences transcend language anyway.

3. TURN OFF YOUR INTERNAL CHATTER. This is very hard to do, especially for those of us who have spent decades learning bad habits. We create a constant play-by-play of our lives, like a TV in the background of our minds that is on all the time. And we're used to it. But to hear, one must be silent. Don't be afraid of silence. Practice stilling your thoughts during meditation and at odd moments of the day. Even doing this for a couple of seconds can bring you closer to the Source. Of course, if you try to describe or categorize the experience into logical, coherent thoughts, you won't be able to. That's the nature of a Mystery, though.

At times you may be able to hear the voice of the Gods. This is very different from the usual chatter of our conscious minds. When, at age sixteen, I told my mother about hearing the voice of the Goddess, her first thought (which she was sweet enough to share with me) was that I must be schizophrenic. In varied indigenous cultures around the world, people who hear voices are respected as seers. But in our society, if you hear something that no one else around you does, it is supposed that something is wrong with you. Yes, there are real psychological disorders, but I believe that some individuals labeled "sick" may just be tied in to a different level of reality, no less real, than the rest of us.

For me, the Goddess will sometimes come through as a sort of wise-ass voice in my mind, cracking jokes at crucial moments.

She often brings me an ironic burst of insight. It's not always something I want to hear, but it rings true. Other times, I will hear words of comfort. When I hear nothing for weeks at a time, I know I have cut myself off from the life-force and I have to find a way to bring my consciousness back to center.

No, I don't really know for certain what it is I'm tapping into. It could be the Goddess, it could be a deeper part of myself, or it could be both. But it doesn't really matter where it comes from; I can tell the difference between that voice and the stray thoughts on the surface of my conscious mind. And intuitively I understand that voice to be powerful and true.

✄ EXERCISE: Sensing the God and Goddess in People

> Day One: Pick someone you care about, someone you know well and respect. While spending time with that person, take a few seconds when they won't notice and just look at them quietly. Think, Thou art God, (or Goddess, depending on the gender). See this person as a perfect image of the Divine. If you want to do this with more than one person, just keep it to people you know well and care about.
>
> Day Two: Try the exercise with random strangers. Make an effort to choose people from different ethnic backgrounds, ages, and people you would generally consider unattractive or even repulsive. Try not to have any expectations about what might happen.
>
> Day Three: Look into a mirror and try the exercise on yourself. This may prove to be a lot harder than you thought. Keep coming back to this one until you really feel like you get it.
>
> On all three days, record what happened in your journal. You might want to do this exercise again in another couple of months and see whether anything has changed.

In this enlightened age, and in this country with freedom of religion, can we find the old Gods again? Most Pagan cultures have been destroyed, and a lot of us have mixed ancestry, so that is why Neo-Pagans have determined to re-create the Gods, in whatever images they reveal themselves.

You can learn all about the Gods from any book on religion or mythology you pick up. You can learn their names, their personalities, their dwelling-places. But Wicca is a shamanic religion that involves the direct experience of Deity. You cannot achieve this through reading.

Don't worry if you still feel unclear about the Gods and how they fit into your life. The Gods may seem like strangers, but they actually dwell within the deepest part of you, and they have been with you all along.

CHAPTER FOUR

Magic

STEPHEN: "My first real experience with magic was most convincing as to its effectiveness. I performed a money ritual and got almost immediate results. While tearing out a bathroom in a house that had just been purchased and was under renovation, I discovered five $20 bills hidden under the light fixture on the medicine cabinet. Coincidence? Luck? Well, yes, but I have found that this is how magic often works. There's always a mundane 'explanation.' "

Many people use the terms *magic* and *Witchcraft* interchangably. But as you already know, Witchcraft is an entire system of beliefs. Magic is an essential *part* of Wicca. Yes, Witches do magic, and although there are no guarantees, magic tends to work more often than it doesn't. It's intriguing to think that you can have absolutely anything you want. But, unfortunately, it's not quite that simple. You have to be sure of what you want, you have to know how to ask for it, you have to know how to help make it happen, and you must be prepared to deal with the consequences when you get it. Nothing in life is free.

What Magic Is and How It Works

Magic is the act of using your will to cause change, by focusing and directing your psychic energy. Writing this book is an act of magic. I visualize the book I want to create, and I make it a reality. If I were to light a candle, burn some incense, and use those images to direct my will to heal a friend, that would be an act of magic as well.

This chapter will focus on using symbols and visualizations to do the second kind of magic, ritual magic. But once you learn to do magic in a ritual setting, you will probably become more aware of how much power you actually possess, all the time. You'll know that you are truly accomplished as a Witch when you realize that any act of will can move mountains—and that sometimes the most powerful magic lies in giving a hug or in picking up trash by the roadside.

In order to understand how magic works, you'll need to examine and probably change your ways of thinking about the concept of magic. "As if by magic" means instant and inexplicable. Just say the right words, mix the right herbs, and POOF!—one person exerts influence over something else, with no physical contact between them.

According to the laws of physics, it is impossible to affect something without physically touching it, so how can I heal my friend who lives halfway across the country? What can bridge the distance?

In some traditions, the problem is solved by Deities. Magic is just another word for prayer. A magician asks a God for a favor in the right way, and the God will hopefully grant his request. The magician is not actually casting the spell himself; he is asking a more powerful being to do the work for him. In such traditions, there need be absolutely no connection between the magician and the object of his spell. They cannot affect each other without using the God as a bridge. The God can affect each of them, because he is all-powerful and doesn't have to worry about limitations of space or time. Now, it's possible (and likely, in my opinion) that in these cases the God is just working as a focus for the individual's power.

Regardless, the official party line is that only Deities can work magic.

For Wiccans, there is no need for a go-between like this, because the separation between things is just an illusion. From the chapter on energy work, you know that all material is, in its most basic state, pure life-energy. This essential force creates an intimate connection between all things. Even the most insignificant thought or action will send ripples of change across the Universe.

But this isn't just philosophy. We can tell from experience that our actions have an impact on the rest of the world. And if you doubt this, take a look around you. If you don't think the things you do can make a difference in your environment, it means you're not taking responsibility for the power and influence you already have! (This point is made in the perennial favorite *It's a Wonderful Life.*)

When you did the exercise in chapter 2, you physically felt the energy that you raised in your hands, so you know that it is not imaginary. You can control it with your will. You can bring it through to the physical plane. "Okay," you say, "How is this tingling in my palms going to get me a new car?" The fact is, it makes no difference whether you're affecting changes in a part of your own body, in another person miles away, or in an event that's going to happen next week. Because psychic energy resides on a deeper level than the physical, it need not follow the physical rules of time and space.

The Steps of Magic

The mechanics of magic happen on the physical plane, but the real work takes place on the spiritual plane. Here are the steps:

Physical	*Spiritual*
• think about what you want to do	• meditate
• plan the mechanics of the spell	• visualize the goal
• gather materials	• raise energy
• do the physical part of the spell	• send out the energy
• clean up and forget about it	• ground and forget about it

When you perform a spell, these steps are intertwined something like this:

- think
- meditate
- visualize
- plan the mechanics
- gather materials
- do the physical part of the spell and raise energy
- send out the energy
- ground
- clean up

When you perform magic, you are working in both worlds at once.

Magic Within Yourself

OBSIDIANA: "I don't like being a victim. I hate the word *victim*. I like being able to take responsibility. Not necessarily control, it's not the same thing. But to be able to take responsibility for what I am. I have no control over a lot of what happens around me, but I have responsibility for what I am."

You can affect others with your magic. But you *must* start with yourself. Just as you must make sure a car is roadworthy before you take it for a drive, before doing magic, you must make sure you are in "working order"—physically, emotionally, and spiritually. No one is expecting you to be perfect, just that you take good care of yourself.

First, your magic will be a lot less effective if you're unhealthy or imbalanced. Second, when you change yourself, you also change things around you. If each individual on Earth decided that he or she personally would not fight in a war, we'd have global peace. Finally, the most important reason to think of yourself first is simply that you deserve it. Some people will say, "You should not use magic for personal gain." I ask, "Why the hell not?" As long as you're not hurting anybody, you should always treat yourself well. And just as you use your hands to make yourself a cup of hot chocolate, so you should use your magical powers to give yourself other things you need or want.

If the concept of will is kind of fuzzy to you, you can think of it here as an element of psychology: the power of positive thinking. Because you're already familiar with this, it's a good place to start from. However, even though magic within yourself is the easiest to understand, in practice it can still be tricky. How many times have you vowed to change something about yourself, really meant it, and then a week or two later you were right back to square one?

Many of us who attempt to diet, for instance, know how frustrating it can be. Why doesn't "willpower" ever seem to work? Here's why: You are mentally splitting yourself in half. Carl Jung talked about the "shadow side" of the personality, made up of elements of yourself that you've labeled bad or wrong. When we diet, we are often fighting the shadow, and the test is to see who will win out. But the separation is an illusion; you are one person. Your different drives and desires are just different parts of you. And when you divorce yourself from the parts of yourself you don't like or approve of, change becomes impossible. If you want to use true willpower, first accept the shadow, and then get in touch with what you truly want (your will). After that, it's a lot easier.

This may seem like a lot of heavy-duty work, and it is. Magic can employ spells, candles, incense, and moonlit forest glades—but it doesn't begin with these. If you cast a spell, it can give you a boost in the direction you want to go. But if, at the same time, you are resisting every step of the way, it just won't work. If I want to get a job, I can do a working—but I'd also better create a good resumé, read the want-ads, and go to interviews. I need to have a clear picture of my goal, and also do the legwork required to get me there. If I don't, the spell may still be effective—but it will probably take longer, fall short, or not turn out the way I really wanted it to.

Non-Pagan friends often ask me for workings: to get a job, get healthy, find romance, you name it. Most of the time I refuse, because I look at what they have been doing for themselves and I know I would be wasting my time. I can tell that even though their conscious mind is asking for it, their inner self would not accept the magic. Believe it or not, people do not always want to be healthy and happy.

You might wonder why anyone would be "content" to be miserable. It's the reason why so many people are content to hand over control of their lives to an outside God. *Power equals responsibility*. If you admit that you are in control of your own fate, that means you have created the bad stuff as well as the good. No complaining is allowed. You are also forced to take your actions very seriously. Consider this: If power over their own life is too great a responsibility for most people to handle, think about what a serious step it is to perform magic that directly affects others!

There is an old tradition in most cultures of having a village wisewoman, or "cunning man," who does the magic for the community. People like to have someone they can go to for help— even if it's just to hear a charm or spell that might work when nothing else has.

If you are the only Witch in your circle of friends, you will be given this role by default. There is no reason not to give magical help when you can. But learn to recognize when the person asking for a spell is trying to skip the "mundane" work himself—or when you feel overburdened—and learn to say a gracious *no* at those times.

> LORRIE: "On several occasions I've had to tell people who want me to do spellwork for them, that I'm not a genie, I'm a Witch."

Magic Affecting Others: Magical Ethics

KRISTINE: "I've talked to a guy who was a deacon in a church, and the first thing he said to me, he kept insisting that it's so easy to get the power and then turn it around and use it for bad. Which I'm sure it is, and I do find myself having to reinforce my own self, because sometimes when I get mad at somebody, I say, 'I should just do *this*,' but then I realize they're going to get theirs in the end as it is. So I don't need to intervene."

There is one very important rule in this kind of magic: *Whatever you do will return to you three times over.* This is known as the "threefold law." (And it doesn't only apply to magic, by the way.) Why does this happen? Spiritually and emotionally speaking, magic is not something you can do from a distance. In order to perform an effective working, you must give yourself over completely to your goal. If you are healing someone, you must overflow with healing energy. If you wish ill on someone, you are going to be filled with destructive energy. You're always essentially performing the spell on yourself first, and then focusing on the other person to send it over. So not only are you affected, but you receive a much stronger dose of the magic than does the second-hand recipient.

When I was fourteen, I cast a love spell on a pen-pal of mine, just as an experiment. I hadn't yet heard about the threefold law. Within a couple of weeks, his letters took a distinctly romantic turn—even mentioning marriage! I became completely obsessed by him, begged my mother to let me go to visit him (to which she predictably replied "Are you kidding?"), and the whole thing was complete chaos. Eventually, things did calm down; after I met a nice local guy whose presence distracted me and dissuaded my pen-pal.

The nice part about the threefold law is that any constructive spells you cast on others also return to you magnified. This brings us to an ethical question: Is it okay to cast spells on others, however positive, without their knowledge or consent? In my tradition, with a few exceptions, the answer is no. Here's why: It's like breaking into a friend's house when she's not home and redecorating her living room. You may do an excellent job, going to a lot of trouble and expense, but it's still an invasion of her space and her privacy—and how do you know she agrees with your choice of wallpaper, or that she wanted the room redecorated in the first place?

The bottom line is, you cannot run other people's lives for them. And there is no way to know what anyone else wants without asking. This goes for healing and protection spells as well. Maybe your elderly grandmother is very sick and tired, at the end of a long struggle with cancer. A "healing" spell might just prolong her pain. It's frustrating to have the power and feel that you shouldn't use it, but magical manipulation is bad karma, and sometimes nonaction can be more helpful than meddling.

> VICTORIA: "Here's the difference between energy and magic. Magic is energy work in a cosmological framework, meaning it's not only 'Gimme what I want.' If it was just energy work, I wouldn't worry about consequences for other people. Because it's spiritual work, I have to be aware of the other people it might affect, the planet, the Universe, etc. I have to look at where the ripples might go. So I have to be a lot more aware of what I'm asking for."

The Nuts and Bolts of Magic

The physical mechanics of a spell (candles, words, tools, etc.) provide a focus for your will. They have no particular power on their own. Many people hold the misconception that any spell in a book was surely put together by an expert, and it has to be done the same way to the letter, or it will fail! In the best of cases, a spell you find in a book will be one that has worked for the person who wrote it. In the worst of cases, it was simply made up to sound impressive.

Contrary to popular belief, symbols are not always universal. If you are doing a working for money, you might choose to use a green candle. Someone else might prefer the color gold for the same spell. This is why I rarely use spells written by other people, because their symbols probably won't match mine exactly—and might actually be very far off!

If a spell you find in a book sounds good to you, go ahead and use it. But you must pay attention to your intuition. *You* are doing the magic, it's *your* will that you want to awaken, and the spell must be one that speaks to *your* subconscious. It really makes much more sense to write your own spells. It's not as hard as you think, and it will be much more effective.

> LORRIE: "My husband was laid off, and we had no income at all. It was winter and we were hungry. The following day he was going deer hunting. I started to do a ritual that included

An altar, set up at a campsite at a Pagan festival. Those are mine and my friends' athames on the right.

sewing a packet filled with luck-related items. While I was sewing I started to hum, no specific song, just humming. I happened to look up at the ceiling when I was sewing the last stitches, and the way the candles were glowing formed a beautiful rack, like a ten-point rack of a stag. I felt warm and safe and confident that what I'd done worked. The following day my husband brought home a six-pointer that fed us the rest of the winter."

Location

For the best results, you should cast a circle before doing spell-work. When you're in circle, you are between the physical and the spiritual world. This offers you access to all realities, all possibilities, and *your goal* on every level of reality. If you were to do spellwork entirely on the physical plane (in the middle of a casual family dinner or while watching TV, for instance), you might have a hard time visualizing or sensing the energy. If you were to try spellwork entirely on the spiritual plane (during a dream, for instance), the energy might be less likely to show up the way you want it to on the physical plane. A sacred circle offers the best of both worlds (so to speak).

Another reason to only perform spellwork in circle is that your energies need to be contained and focused. A circle also provides a boundary. When you want to lend more volume to your voice, you can cup your hands around your mouth. If you want to keep the heat inside a room, you must keep the door closed. When you cast a spell, you will release psychic energy toward your goal, without some kind of container, the energy will fly out in all directions and be much less useful, if not completely ineffective.

That boundary is also necessary for protection. Due to the kind of concentration and receptivity required for any kind of energy work, you will be somewhat vulnerable. At such times you are much more likely to encounter energy fluctuations that will be, at best, distracting, and, at worst, may leave you drained.

Planning Your Spell

Two major concerns in spell-planning are ethics and practicality. Of the two, ethics are much more important. Is this spell necessary? What do I *really* want? How will it affect my life and that of those around me? Will the results be compatible with my personal principles? Can I live with the threefold payback? After you've gone through all that, you have the practical concern of making sure the spell will work. After the perplexing ethical questions, this part is a breeze, and can be done through trial and error. (Trial-and-error ethics would be a bad thing.)

You also might want to consider the astrological conditions. Many Wiccans want to make sure the "correspondences" are right before they cast any particular spell—the moon should be in the proper phase, the time of day must be correct, and so forth. I've never had much of an interest in astrology and confess to being somewhat skeptical about its effectiveness. But if you are mindful of the planetary positions, by all means work this knowledge into your magic. If you are not, don't worry about it. I believe that what you don't know (in this case) won't affect you.

Start with a piece of paper and a pen. Begin with your goal (write it in big letters at the top of the page). Write your goal in the center of the piece of paper, referring to it as a current reality. "I AM HEALTHY!", for instance. Then assemble a list of things—objects, feelings, ideas, colors—that you associate with that goal. Don't worry about practicality. You're brainstorming. If you want to use the Atlantic Ocean, write it down. You can always modify it down to a seashell and some saltwater later. The actual materials you use are not as important as the strength of the associations that you have with them.

Write only those things that have meaning for you personally. For instance, if you've never understood why the owl should be used as a symbol for wisdom, don't use that animal. Find another one that works for you. If the images you come up with seem silly, write them down anyway. They might be surprisingly effective. Why not use Yoda as a symbol for wisdom? No one's saying you have to *use* every idea, anyway.

Now you have a piece of paper with a lot of words, pictures, and symbols. You *can* use this as a focus for the spell. However, it's kind of abstract. It's often more effective to use something you can do in the physical world that will mirror your magical action. So take a look at what you've written or drawn. How can you bring this into the physical world? For instance, if you thought of the color green, light a green candle. A spell for health could involve a couple of vitamin C tablets—and if it's for you, you could take them at the end! A spell to bring money to you could involve some shiny coins.

Candles make an especially good focus because a lot of people already associate them with magic and mystery. You might want to rub a scented oil onto the candle, light the candle while saying a few powerful words, and then let it burn down to cement the spell. You could also carve images into the candle beforehand (like a heart for love). These are all pretty obvious ideas—doubtless there will be some symbols that have a very strong meaning for you alone. Use them.

As far as materials for spellwork go, some day you must find a certain herb, gemstone, or use only sterling silver tools—and if you don't get these exact materials, your spell won't work. There are no rules or regulations about what you are "allowed" or "supposed" to use. If you don't have access to a metaphysical supply shop, or if you don't want to have the stuff lying around where it might be seen by people who don't understand, just improvise. One of the simplest spells can be done by visualizing your goal, focusing the energy, pouring it into a glass of water or juice as you hold it in both hands, and then drinking it down. No weird paraphernalia, just pure and simple intent.

Intent and Focus

The way you focus your mind is what makes the difference between just having some orange juice, and drinking down a spell. You've got your props, your script, your circle is cast, and you're standing in the middle of the room. What's going on inside your head? If you're thinking about anything except the goal of your spell, it won't work. When you visualize, you are thinking about one thing, one image, one idea or feeling, and you see it crystal clear.

If you want to shoot something with a bow and arrow, you don't just point in its general direction and hope you get lucky. You must shut out everything except that thing you want to hit, line up your arrow, draw back, and let go. If you don't aim correctly, no amount of strength in your bow will make up for it.

When you're doing celebratory ritual, it's not a big deal if your thoughts wander; you just gently bring them back. But in spell-work, there's more at stake. If you lose focus, at best your spell will be less effective. At worst, if your focus turns negative, you may give energy to your fears and anxieties and make them stronger.

It will be easier to keep your focus if you practice the relaxation/meditation techniques, use just a couple of very meaningful props, and keep the goal of the spell very simple and specific. Still, it is impossible to predict the way a spell will turn out. I heard of someone who did a spell for "lots of money" and ended up working in a bank. This is an example of the Gods' sense of humor. Not all magical mishaps are so harmless, however. He might have had a much loved older relative die and leave him a fortune. It's imporant to be very, very specific about the desired outcome. With magic, you will *always* get exactly what you ask for—not always what you need or want.

> VICTORIA: "I would never do a love spell for a specific person. You could be messing with their free will, but that's not the point. The point is I need love and affection, and that could come from more than one specific person."

Ask yourself if your goal is a means or an end. For example, you may want a large amount of money. Understandable! But money is rarely an end in itself; it's usually a means to get something else: possessions, security, popularity, and so forth. What do you *really* want?

Also, keep focused on something positive. Try repeating this phrase in your mind for a few times: "I am not upset." That may seem like a positive thought at first, but all your subconscious hears is the word "upset," and it responds accordingly. Instead, try repeating "I am calm and happy."

Even if the spell is for something that has not yet happened, it is important that you phrase the words as if it's happening right now. Magically speaking, time is meaningless. When you do a spell, you are creating a reality. You need to be as close to that reality as possible. It is much more powerful to say "I am being promoted at work," than "Next month, I will be promoted at work." It doesn't matter that you won't even have your review for three weeks. The magical push starts now.

Power-Raising

In order to give a spell that push it needs, it is necessary to gather and direct energy. This is frequently referred to as raising and sending power. It often happens naturally in celebratory rituals where there is drumming or dancing, but in spellwork, the power raised makes the magic more effective. Remember, for personal safety and health, the energy for this must be drawn up from the Earth and grounded again afterward.

Different methods for raising power work for different people. Some find a certain type of music or chanting effective, others may dislike noise and prefer yogic breathing techniques. The kind of power-raising should also change depending on your mood and the purpose of the spell. A healing for a small child might call for a gentle, quiet chant, whereas a prosperity spell could be louder and more aggressive.

To raise power, take a deep breath and feel yourself drawing energy up from the Earth. Give it a few seconds; it won't happen instantaneously. You are raising your own energy frequency. You are gathering together the magical materials for the spell. When you inhale, your power grows.

At this time, you might feel your heartbeat quickening, or you may slip into a slight trance. A lot of people start to feel the energy coming out of their palms and feet, and feel their whole body buzzing. Your aura will grow and you may sense it becoming brighter. Whatever happens, try to keep your focus on the intent of the spell. When the energy gets as high as it's going to go, release it. See it spiraling upward. Let go of your focus; forget about your intent. If you cling to it and dwell on it after you have sent off the power, you will weaken the spell.

What can you do if you change your mind about a spell, or if it goes wrong? Is there any way to "take it back"? Unfortunately, no. Spells work like anything else. If you accidentally bump into someone and bruise him, you can apologize, you can give him some ice to put on his injury, you can promise never to do it again, but the deed has been done. The bruise stays. You should never do a spell you haven't thought through completely, but if you do cast a spell and immediately regret it, you can try doing another working to counteract it before it hits. This doesn't usually work, however, because the ripples have already been set in motion. What will probably happen is the first spell will hit, and then the second spell will go into effect on top of it—a waste of time that may just make things worse.

You should expect to screw up at first. Any new skill takes time to learn. There are so many variables that mishaps are practically guaranteed. But don't let your fears or misgivings keep you from doing magic. It can be very useful if things go wrong, because that will teach you what *not* to do next time.

Once you start learning how to do magic—and there's really no way to learn but to just start doing it—your life will change dramatically. As long as you stay grounded, stay honest with yourself and considerate of those you may be affecting, the changes will be positive. But be warned: Magic is not meant to be a hobby. It's real, it works, and it's rarely predictable.

CHAPTER FIVE

The Sabbats

Toм: "It was Samhain of 1993, and I was doing a banishing ritual . . . releasing all my exes from past relationships. I carried with me photos and memorabilia that were my connections to those people. It was about three or four in the afternoon, so the sun was still out. The four of us were going into the woods behind my friend's house, and we were looking for a place to build a fire, to burn these things and release them. By the time we'd gathered up some wood and started it, it was already getting dark, and we had a pretty good blaze going. And I started throwing photos and things in the fire, and saying, 'This is Samhain, this is the season of winter, this is the time to get rid of those things in your life that still haunt you. . . .' and it was really powerful, I felt the release of this burden come off my shoulders. After it was done, it had to be about eight at night—so this was over the course of four or five hours—and there was sort of a light mist all around the woods, and it was light enough so you could see your way back, so it was as if the Gods lit my way back. It was as if I had taken a journey into the otherworld and came back."

Sabbats are sacred days, the spokes around the wheel of the year. While the holidays of most "mainstream" traditions generally commemorate one-time-only historic events, such as Christmas, Passover, and Thanksgiving, the sacred days of Wicca and other nature religions are meant to celebrate the changes in the earth that happen *every* year.

Most scholars believe that our modern religious holidays are based on Pagan precedents. In that way, they *are* tied in to the seasons. "Easter" and "springtime" are inexorably linked. But for people who practice Christiantiy, the event (Jesus rising from the dead) comes first—and any connection it has to springtime is just something we humans added on later to make it more meaningful for us. The thing they are celebrating is the resurrection of their savior, not the rebirth of Nature. If anything, Nature is mirroring the historic event by coming alive! These traditions tend to view history as a straight line, extending from creation to the end of the world.

But to the Pagan, whose inspiration comes from Nature rather than from the pages of a book, this just doesn't make sense. It is impossible to create something from nothing. Likewise, it is impossible to truly destroy anything. *Things simply change form, and the only constant is change.* One Pagan chant goes, "We are a circle within a circle, with no beginning and never ending." The sprout that comes from the earth has its origins in the fallen tree before it, which came from a sprout.

The eight sabbats of the Wiccan year represent that cycle of life. Together, they are sometimes referred to as the Wheel of the Year. The sabbats, or the spokes of the wheel, are the solstices, the equinoxes, and the halfway points between each of them. By acknowledging those points, we are actually celebrating the continuity of the entire cycle. It goes as follows:

- *Samhain,* November 1 (halfway between autumn and winter)
- *Yule,* December 20–23 (winter solstice)
- *Imbolc,* February 2 (halfway between winter and spring)
- *Ostara,* March 20–23 (spring equinox)
- *Beltane,* May 1 (halfway between spring and summer)
- *Litha,* June 20–23 (summer solstice)

- *Lughnassadh,* August 1 (halfway between summer and autumn)
- *Mabon,* September 20–23 (autumn equinox)

All of these holidays are rooted in ancient European history. It's worth noting, though, that different traditions either marked the solstices and equinoxes, or just the cross-quarters—Samhain, Imbolc, Beltane, and Lughnassadh. Wicca is the first religion ever to observe all eight.

The Celts were one group that placed emphasis on those "cross-quarters." Since Wicca takes a large part of its inspiration from that culture, those holidays are considered the greater sabbats. This is not to say that they are any more sacred than the other four; but more emphasis is placed on celebrating them. These sabbats also tend to be more complex, being a combination of two seasons. For instance, Samhain is a combination of autumn and winter, so it is a harvest holiday, full of bounty and celebration, but there is an edge of cold beneath the surface, foreshadowing the dark winter to come.

The pattern of the seasons is always the same. Fallen leaves in autumn have *always* smelled sweet and earthy. When the crocuses appear, the trees will soon be bursting with leaves. Snow will crunch beneath a walker's feet, and then it will melt. The cycle is a constant; each season blends seamlessly into another, and it never ends. The wheel is always turning. We celebrate the sabbats to ensure that we stay connected with what is going on around us—and that we are always changing and moving along with the Earth. Within every sabbat is the seed of its opposite. So we celebrate the changes completely and with a whole heart, but we stay mindful that nothing is permanent except change.

VICTORIA: "The way we celebrate the sabbats should reflect our own position with respect to the issue that the sabbat brings up. On the other hand, we do need to stay connected with what's going on with the planet on a larger scale and not turn it into a group therapy session. It needs to be a balance between our personal needs and what's going on in the cycle of the Earth."

The idea of "Nature" as a separate entity is really an illusion. Our shivering bodies are just as much a part of Nature as are the chill winds. And the changes in the Earth bring changes in us. When it's cold and dark outside, people get more quiet and introspective. Then people begin to feel more energetic and playful as the days get warmer and longer. When we celebrate the sabbats, we are nurturing that connection.

Some covens celebrate the sabbats on the closest Saturday to the date (sometimes that's the only day they can get everyone together.) Others are very precise in their timing, taking into account the fact that the astrological dates of the sabbats actually change every year. You will want to go to the trouble of doing your sabbat rituals on the precise date (astrological or traditional), if doing so will make it a more meaningful and intense experience. I try to make the timing of my ritual a conscious thing, not subject to when it is most convenient for me. This may mean staying up late on a weeknight when I have to go to work bleary-eyed the next day, but I prefer to make as few compromises as possible in practicing my Craft. Of course, this may be what I prefer, but, well, life happens.

So let's say it's a sabbat today, but you have a test to prepare for, or your best (non-Pagan) friend is visiting, or you're sick, or you're just not in the mood. What happens if you don't do anything to observe the occasion? First of all, you are not a "better" Witch if you observe the sabbats than if you don't. Your practice of the Craft is about how you live your life, not how often you cast a circle. And there is no heavenly authority obliging you to hold rituals for every sabbat, so there's no point in feeling guilty if you don't.

And if you ignore one or two? Amazingly enough, the Earth keeps right on turning. But especially if you're just starting in the Craft, you might want to try to observe all the sabbats in some way. It will help to make your practice a more important part of your life and to cement your sense of commitment. You may not think that it would make a difference, but try one year of passionate involvement with the changes in the Earth, and then skip a couple of sabbats. You will start to feel disconnected and a little out of touch. And you will realize the joy you had felt when you were following the wheel of the year.

Observing the sabbats doesn't always mean writing, choreographing, and performing a glamorous ritual. It can be as simple as meditating on a symbol of the season or going for a quiet walk in the woods. It doesn't matter exactly what you do—if you have decided it is a sabbat ritual, then it is.

> LORRIE: "I celebrate the sabbats within my home by letting everyone know the history of that day. By reading something aloud to my family and telling friends who aren't Pagan that today is a holiday for me. I decorate my kitchen table or entertainment center for that specific sabbat. Then late at night I take a cleansing bath or shower and proceed with the ritual for that sabbat."

Many of the sabbats are still observed unintentionally by people in this country. Samhain has become Halloween, Yule has become Christmas and Chanukah, Imbolc has become Groundhog Day, Ostara has become Easter, Beltane has become May Day, and Mabon has become Thanksgiving. If you are feeling isolated in your celebrations, try to notice the elements of the old holidays peeking through the new. If you look into the eyes of the baby Jesus in a creche, you may see the newborn sun at solstice time.

Samhain, November 1

As do the ceremonial dates in many religious traditions, sabbats actually begin at sundown the previous day. That's why we are used to celebrating Samhain as All Hallows' Eve on October 31. The Catholic church placed All Souls' Day on the date of the actual sabbat, November 1.

Samhain is at the same time the death of the old year and the birth of the new. There is a fine line between birth and death—they are both transitions into a completely unknown world.

Samhain is truly a sabbat of transitions, because it is also the time the division between the world of form and the world of spirit grows thin. The astral body is less bound to the physical, so astral travel is easier. We can also invite those from the other side to visit us here, and that is why ghosts are associated with Halloween.

Samhain is a time to remember and connect with our ancestors, as well as with people we have known and loved who have passed over to the other side. You may not literally see your late grandma cooking in your kitchen, but you might catch a whiff of her perfume—or suddenly remember something funny she used to do. If someone you care about has died in the past year, take a few minutes to remember them and maybe say hello. Remember that the dead are *invited*, not summoned.

Samhain is considered by some to be the most important sabbat. This is because it represents the core experiences of the Craft: of traveling between the worlds, of experiencing death and rebirth, and of ultimately transcending both in the process; of not being afraid to face the darkness, or to think about that which we have lost; of not being afraid of the changes in our lives; of turning negative experiences into opportunities for learning.

The darkness is growing. At Samhain, we are heading into the gloomiest time of the year, but Samhain is not all gloom and doom. One of the most important magical concepts is that everything contains within it the seed of its opposite. Many of those elements of the old holiday which survived—jack-o'-lanterns, silly costumes, pranks—seem to contradict the somber nature of Samhain. They are the life within death. Death and cold are grim realities. We accept them wholeheartedly, but we can always use some comic relief. Many Pagans celebrate the sabbat alone or with their coven, and then go to parties or costume balls on the weekend.

Because of the significance of "life in death," sexual power is very important at this time. To make love is traditional on Beltane, the rowdy spring sabbat—but it is even more important on Samhain. For what better way could there be to honor life at a time of death? Feasting and celebration are a way of demonstrating our trust that there will be enough bounty to see us through the winter.

Samhain is an excellent time for divination and other magical work. Since the veil between worlds is thin, people's psychic and magical abilities become stronger. The growing dark and cold also encourage introspection, as the season drives us deeper into ourselves. This can manifest as moodiness or a somber feeling. If it doesn't get too extreme, let it happen. Any kind of effective magical work must begin with self-exploration and self-knowledge. The hag, the Crone, the Halloween Witch, the 'shadow' exists within all of us. She isn't evil, she's just dark, mysterious and powerful, unpredictable, and a bit chaotic. That part of us contains a lot of our power.

Traditional for Samhain: Pumpkins, the color black, the moon, pomegranates, skulls, any form of divination.

Yule, December 20–23

At Samhain we were beginning to turn toward the dark, to start our journey into the underworld. Now we are in the midst of it—underground, in the heart of the darkness, the longest night. It seems as if the sun has left forever, and in some prehistoric cultures there probably was a real fear that it wouldn't return.

And so we strike flames to encourage the sun. We gather together with our friends and feast, drink hot cider, make our own heat where the Earth provides none. One beauty of the longest night is that it marks the beginning of the sun's return. Every sabbat contains its opposite, and there is a hint of summer solstice in the center of the cold we feel right now.

Yule is another time of death and rebirth. The God of growing light, the Oak King, is born and slays the God of fading light, the Holly King. Light triumphs over darkness, and the balance shifts.

The sun God returns at winter solstice, and the foundation of the modern celebration of Christmas can be traced to ancient Yultide traditions. Decorating an evergreen, burning a Yule log, singing carols, hanging lights—all were Pagan Yuletide customs. Even Santa Claus can be seen as the old and dying God, the Holly King. You shouldn't be shy about observing "Christmas" traditions. More likely than not, they were Pagan first. Just smile and call that decorated evergreen a "seasonal shrub."

Traditional for Yule: Evergreen trees; holly; ivy; mistletoe; candles; spices such as cloves, cinnamon, and nutmeg; citrus fruit (reminders of the sun); the colors red, green, silver, and gold.

Imbolc, February 2

As hard as it may be to believe it, in the midst of snow and ice, this is the very beginning of spring. The name *Imbolc* (originally Imbolg) means "in the belly": the quickening of spring in the belly of the Earth. Beneath the ground, seeds are stirring. At Imbolc, tiny buds can sometimes be seen on certain trees. But even when there is no visible sign of spring, we have faith in the cycle of the seasons, knowing that the cold will soon be behind us.

All Yule decorations must traditionally be thrown out or packed away before this day. To keep them up is to invite bad luck. We must not cling to winter, but instead welcome the spring.

February can be a very depressing month. It's dark and cold. The snow that seemed so beautiful in December now presents nothing but a dirty gray obstacle, as we dig our cars out and take care not to slip on the icy sidewalks. But we must look ahead to the warmth and healing power of the sun. The days getting longer and the sun is growing stronger.

This holiday is sacred to the Goddess Brigid (pronounced "breed"), who is associated with poetry, healing, and smithcraft. As part of a sabbat celebration, you may wish to try your hand at poetry, which comes from a deeper place than ordinary speech or writing. Allow Brigid to be your muse. Go within yourself and see what she shows you.

As for healing—what do you need to heal in your life? How are you going to do it? This doesn't have to include just psychic or spiritual matters. When we are forced inside, forced to slow down, forced to endure the darkness and cold, it can be seen as a time to heal ourselves. Then we can enter into the springtime renewed.

And smithcraft: The symbolism of fire, and the forge, is very complex. Fire transforms. If you put a piece of wood into fire, it will become ash, and blow away. But if you put a piece of metal, such as iron, into the searing heat, it will become stronger and more pliable. The forge of the Goddess Brigid is a place of transformation and strength. All the sabbats are about change, because they are spokes on the wheel of the year that is always moving. But transformation is different than simple change. It is about becoming something, or someone, totally new—and stronger.

Traditional for Imbolc: Milk, candles, fire, the forge, iron, the written word, the colors white and yellow.

Ostara, March 20–23

Ostara falls on the spring equinox. The ground is still a dull brown-gray, the temperatures are in the forties, and there is a possibility of snow for the end of the week. How can we celebrate the first day of spring if it still feels like winter?

Being a Witch means looking beneath the surface. Poking up through the still-barren ground are the hopeful shoots of early flowers, and it's beginning to smell like spring outdoors. The sabbats are markers to help people honor these constant subtle changes in the Earth.

Ostara stems from the name of a Teutonic Goddess, "Eostre." It's not accidental that the name sounds suspiciously like a Christian holiday that's celebrated around this time. Again, the new religion "borrowed" from the old.

Equinoxes are times of balance between light and darkness, when day and night are of equal length. You might want to try the old trick of standing an egg on end at the precise moment of the equinox. Balance your own energies along with it.

The egg—that powerful symbol—is almost universally understood to represent fertility, rebirth, and resurrection. After Ostara, that which was "in the belly" at Imbolc is finally born. The world comes back to life. How are you being reborn? How are you a brand-new person? Come out of your winter cocoon and start spending more time outside.

> JUDY: "In many ways, the more interesting sabbat customs are the ones that each coven or household develops for itself —these are the ones that give us a sense of 'us-ness.' For example, my coven has a custom of eating ginger at the vernal equinox (Ostara). This started when my partner and I were doing a call-in radio show. A caller recommended crystallized ginger as a spring tonic. One of our coven members was listening. It sounded like a good idea to him, so he brought some to the ritual. We were delighted, and it became one of our regular 'things.' "

The balance shifts. Light is mastering the darkness. Winter is truly over. Celebrate!

Traditional for Ostara: Eggs, rabbits, flowers, baby animals—all symbolic of fertility and new life. The four-leaf clover and hot cross buns, which represent balance and wholeness. The colors green, for plants, and red, for the blood of life.

Beltane, May 1

Ask any Witch what her favorite sabbat is, and most of them will probably answer "Beltane." This is traditionally the wedding day of the God and Goddess—and anyone who's been to an ethnic wedding knows what a wild party it can be. Beltane is a day devoted to flirtations, to courting, and to falling in love. Spring has  arrived, and it's picking up momentum. Beltane is the moment before orgasm—which can sometimes be sweeter than the climax itself.

Beltane is an unashamedly sexual sabbat. Traditionally, on May Eve (the night before), couples would take to the woods and fields to make love. This was meant to encourage the crops to grow. That's known as sympathetic magic; the fertility of a couple would bring fertility to the fields. But even before that tradition got started, I imagine the revelers were simply acting out the sacred marriage of the Lord and Lady.

On the other hand:

VICTORIA: "On Beltane, if you don't have a partner, it can be lonely and frustrating. If you're with someone and not getting along with them, or if you're in a sexual slump with your partner, it's going to create tension. So what my coven did, when we did the maypole ritual, was to focus on the union of God and Goddess, and to have a more contemplative experience. It was more quietly sensual on a cosmic scale, as opposed to, 'Gee, let's go around and kiss somebody.' The feedback we got from the community was actually a lot of relief. A lot of the Beltanes in the past had been really hot and sexy. People appreciated having something different every year. God and Goddess manifest love and lust in infinite ways. So having a sedate Beltane is not necessarily out of rhythm with the God and Goddess."

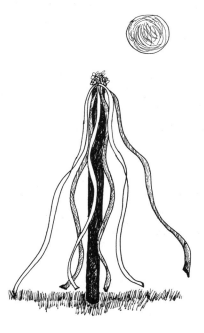

The maypole and the rite surrounding it are part of the few Pagan traditions that have been preserved unaltered through the centuries. Of course, the symbolism of the huge erect pole being stuck into a hole in the earth is pretty obvious. The dancers adorn the symbolic phallus of the God with ribbons. The ribbons wind around the pole and spiral down to the earth, drawing the renewing energy of the Sky God down into the receiving body of the Earth Goddess. Again, participants are acting out the sacred marriage— and even assisting in the mechanics.

Beltane is one of the fire festivals, and bonfires (also called bel-fires) are traditional. Fire is associated with sexual passion, with transformation and renewal. It is also customary to leap over a bonfire on Beltane. This can be done to bless a relationship or to bring fertility. More recently, Wiccans tend to use the cleansing power of the flames to burn away unwanted influences. The fire can be seen as a sacrificial pyre; throw what you don't want anymore (simply visualized, or written on a piece of paper) into the flames. If you can't have a bonfire, a candle will suffice.

Traditional for Beltane: Bright colors (especially red and white), fruit, flowers, music and dance, expressions of love.

Litha, June 20–23

If Beltane is foreplay, Litha (more commonly called Midsummer) is the orgasm. Everything is peaking; the world seems to have erupted in green. It may not be the hottest day of the year, but it is the one with the most hours of sunlight. This is the extent of the sun's power, the peak of the God of the growing light, the Oak King.

The term *Midsummer* might seem odd, as this date is now considered the beginning of summer. But the ancient Celts had only two seasons: light and dark, summer and winter. This is actually the middle of the light half of the year. Now, after the sun's peak, the growing light begins to fade. This is the return of the darkness.

That's right, even as you make your beach-party plans, the God of the fading light, the Holly King, will slay the Oak King and will regain his power. The days will grow shorter and the nights longer.

But this is *not* a somber holiday. That coming darkness is just the briefest note in the celebration of Midsummer, as we rejoice in the extreme abundance of the Earth.

Midsummer, like Beltane, is a fire festival. The bonfire mirrors the powerful sun. Again, we jump the bonfire (or pass between lit candles) to infuse ourselves with that power—as well as to symbolically burn away what we don't need.

The idea of Gods killing each other isn't just an entertaining story, it's a powerful magical image. When the Holly King slays the Oak King, it isn't a literal death; it means a shift in the balance of power. The Oak King has simply left the scene until he can return again. This mirrors the Wiccan concept that death is neither "bad" or "evil," rather a necessary transition, a shift into another form.

Traditional for Midsummer: bonfires, the sun, flowers (especially red heather), fruit, water, the color green.

Lughnassadh, August 1

This is the first of the harvest holidays. It's pronounced "LOO-nu-sutch, LOO-na-say, or loo-NA-suh, depending on who you talk to. Or you can just use "Lammas," a more recent deriva-  tion of the word. (I still laugh when I think of my mother asking incredulously, "You worship *llamas*?")

The holiday, like Brigid, is named after a Deity—in this case, Lugh, a Celtic God of sun and fire. Because the sun's light is beginning to fade, Lughnassadh is actually the day of his demise.

It is not a sad occasion, however. Without the harvest, without death, no one will be fed; there can be no new life. When Lugh is sacrificed, we reap the bounty. The crucifixion of Jesus is actually a later version of the same idea: Death and sacrifice bring new life. The cycle is eternal. The theme is played out in the Christian year, if observed as a cycle: Jesus is continually dying and being reborn, only to die again. In Paganism, it is only fitting that the death of the God must come with the harvest.

Because of this, grain is an important symbol at Lughnassadh, and baking bread is traditional at this time. I once participated in a powerful ritual, in which every participant took a turn kneading the bread dough and keeping up a continuous chant. Lugh (symbolized by the bread) rose once, and was beaten down. He rose again, and was beaten down. He rose a third time, and that time he entered the oven (symbolic of sexually entering the Goddess).

He came out transformed from this final death. We all ate the bread and took in the blessing of new life.

Lughnassadh is a summer sabbat. The sun is still burning brightly and the entire world seems draped in green. This is not a time for dwelling on the fading light, it is a time for celebration of the bounty we see all around us. Many covens hold their Lughnassadh circles outdoors, and the group I was trained in has a traditional water-gun fight after the completion of the ritual. Lugh is slain, but in that sacrifice he burns his brightest light.

Traditional for Lughnassadh: Grain, bread, corn, sun, fire, the color yellow.

Mabon, September 20–23

Mabon is the autumn equinox. Like Ostara, it is a time of perfect balance between light and dark, but this time it is the darkness that will grow. Mabon is a harvest holiday, like Lughnassadh, but without the glorious sun-related imagery. The mood here is more somber. This is the completion, the end of the harvest. The American Thanksgiving is supposed to be a harvest holiday, but it's so late in the season that the actual harvest is long over and it's already starting to feel like winter. At Mabon, we are still trying to eat our way through the tomatoes and zucchini that we are overly blessed with every late summer. It's about bounty!

In ancient times, this was the day when farmers settled their debts with the landowners. Both equinoxes are times of balance, but Mabon is a time of *rebalancing*; of setting things right. The harvest is collected, and it is time to take stock of what we have. Giving thanks is not just about being grateful, it also involves assessment and contemplation.

The symbol of the grain, important at Lughnassadh, is still relevant at Mabon. However, it is no longer a glorious celebration of bounty. Life is slowing down, and more attention is paid to the idea of death and rebirth. The Eleusinian Mysteries of ancient Greece were performed at this time. Initiates would be shown a

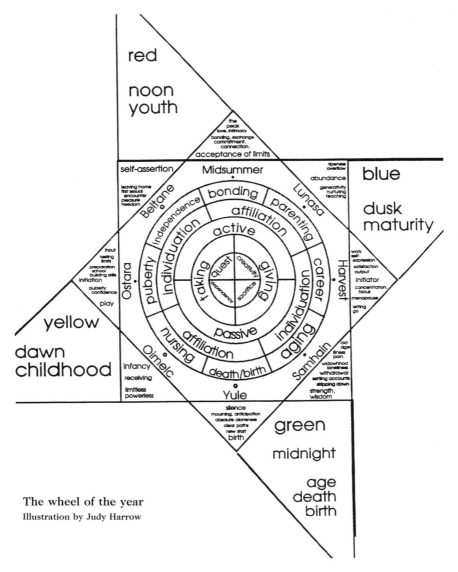

The wheel of the year
Illustration by Judy Harrow

single ear of grain, and told, "In silence is the seed of wisdom gained." Mabon is the beginning of the silence that comes with the dark half of the year.

Traditional for Mabon: Grain, late summer vegetables, forest green and earth tones.

The sabbats are days when we renew our connection with the Earth. The holidays described above come from the Celtic tradition, but in modern Wicca they cross all ethnic boundaries. They are the points we choose to mark on the wheel of the year. The basic symbolism—the sun's death and rebirth, the bounty of spring, the celebration of the harvest—these are common to almost all civilizations.

As you celebrate the sabbats, you'll find that they mean different things to you each year—and you will learn new things each time. One Samhain may be an emotional farewell to a dear friend or relative, and another may be a wild vampirelike spin on the dark side of life. The effect the sabbats have will change, but the basic symbolism remains constant. In that way, we are able to grow and learn within the wheel of the year, and still feel safe within the cradle of the Earth Mother, feeling the seasons come and go.

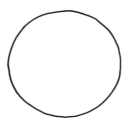

Part Two

The Mother
Moving Between the Worlds

We call on you, O Mother,
As she who knows, and understands;
We feel your warm protective arms around us,
We feel the solid Earth beneath.
You, who bring all things to fruitfulness,
You, who birth the world from your womb,
Bring to us the bounty of your garden,
Teach us where the center still remains.

CHAPTER SIX

Magical Tools and Altars

CATHERINE: "When I was about twelve years old, when I had my first period, around that time was when I made my first tools. I made my first athame (ritual knife) out of wood. I didn't know what I was making. It wasn't until I read *The Spiral Dance* when I was thirty, that I saw the description of tools and said, 'I have this, I have that,' and I had a name for things."

Magical tools may be used in ritual, to help ground or move energy, or in the context of a spell. However, depending on the kind of magic you practice, they may function solely as symbols. They can be kept on your altar to represent the four elements, and they can be used in meditations as images to focus on.

The basic magical tools are:

Athame. This is traditionally a small double-bladed dagger. It represents the direction of east, and the power of air. The athame is masculine and is generally used for directing and moving energy. You can use your athame as an extension of yourself, to cast a circle, cut a gateway in a circle, or to bless an object or a food. Your athame does not have to be an elaborate work of art. A kitchen knife is just as effective as a $300-handcrafted dagger, and I knew someone whose athame was a Swiss Army knife.

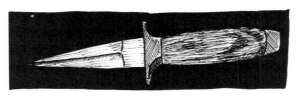

Traditionally, athames are not supposed to be used to cut anything physical. There is sometimes also a white-handled knife, meant for cutting herbs and such—Craft-related things. I don't own one, so I have used my athame in that capacity. At any rate, it should be stressed here that athames are absolutely never used to harm any living thing.

People often go off the deep end when they see my athame on my altar, imagining bloody sacrifices, or other images out of horror movies. These fears are easily put to rest by a few minutes of explanation. But the fact remains that the athame is a weapon. The blade is supposed to be sharp. (I was in a working group with a woman who refused to use an athame because it was a weapon. I did not try to force her around to my way of thinking, but I did stop doing magic with her.) True, you can inflict harm with an athame. But our own hands can be used as weapons. And isn't magic the most powerful—and dangerous—weapon of all? The sharp edge of the blade is a reminder of the power we take into our hands when we work magic.

How do you go about finding an athame? If you want something prettier than a Swiss Army knife and a little more special, you can look around at Renaissance fairs. I was fortunate enough to find an inexpensive dagger at such an event that, years later, still serves me just fine. If you are under eighteen, you may encounter some trouble in purchasing a knife. Also, in some states, double-bladed knives are illegal. I have seen people use pointed stones or crystals as a substitute. If you just can't find anything that suits you as an athame, wait. It will find you at the right time.

Wand. The wand is associated with the south, and the power of fire. Like the athame, it is also sometimes used for moving energy. I cast circles with my wand before I got my athame. There are no rules about what material a wand should be made from. It can be wood, metal, glass, stone—I know someone who used a plastic glitter-filled "magic" wand. Traditionally, it should measure the same distance as from your fingertips to your elbow, but that's mainly for the sake of utility. And if it's really big, it should be considered a staff!

My wand, which I made at age sixteen, was the first tool I owned. I went into the woods across the street, and it didn't take long for me to find a small stick that was exactly the right length, with a beautiful curve. I took it home, peeled off the bark, whittled it, and sanded it down. I carved my magical name into it, and a pretty pentacle near the tip, and glued an amethyst onto it. It still sits on my altar. I have never needed another one.

New Age shops often have extremely fancy wands, costing hundreds of dollars. Sometimes people value something more if they spend a lot of money for it. If you're that kind of person, save up your money and treat yourself to an original work of art. I've never had occasion to use one of these wands, but I imagine they work just about the same thing as my sweet little wooden one. (Can you guess that I'm a bit biased toward the homemade approach?)

On that note, you can also just pick up a stick from the woods and bring it home to use as your wand, without doing a single thing to "pretty it up." Sometimes simple is best.

Chalice. This cup, glass, or goblet is associated with the west, and the power of water. It is a feminine tool. You may have noticed that the masculine tools are long and thin, very directed in shape, and that this feminine one is more curved and receptive. Just as the male tools are phallic (representing the penis, the male element), the female tools are shaped according to their feminine correspondences. The chalice is round and hollow, like a belly, or a womb. When it is filled with wine, juice, water, or milk, it becomes an even more potent Goddess symbol. In ritual, when we take a sip from the chalice, we are partaking of the bounty of the Goddess.

You can also use your chalice as a scrying tool. The element of water has long been associated with the subconscious, with dreams, with emotions, and with psychic ability. Just fill the cup with a dark liquid—such as grape juice, red wine, or even colored water—and look into it in a dimly lit room, allowing your thoughts to drift and your eyes to become unfocused. Open yourself up to any images that may come to you.

Considering how relatively inexpensive they are, chalices are beautiful and satisfying tools to purchase. For under twenty dollars, you can usually find beautiful handmade ceramic cups at any craft fair or Renaissance festival. Of course, the chalice can be made of any material, including glass or wood. Beware of pretty pewter cups; pewter contains lead and is not always safe to drink from. It's best to use them only as decoration. If you are planning group work, get yourself a large chalice so you don't have to keep refilling it as it passes around the circle.

Pentacle. This is traditionally a flat stone or metal disk, usually with a five-pointed star inscribed upon it. It is associated with the north, and the element of earth. Smooth, rounded, and receptive, it is also a female symbol. It can be used for grounding stray energy in a room. You can also grab hold of it when you are stressed out or upset and pour your emotions into it. Just remember to place it on the ground afterward so the negative energy can be recycled by the Earth.

"Pentacles" and "pentagrams" are sometimes confused. A pentacle is three-dimensional and is made of metal, stone, wood, or clay. It can be an adornment or a part of your altar. A pentagram is the same five-pointed star, but it is either drawn on a flat surface or traced by movement of a finger, wand, or athame. It is two-dimensional—not an object.

> LAUREL: "I had always wanted my pentacle as a gift, I felt that was the way it should be. And nobody got the hint, and I didn't want to buy my own. I also didn't want it till I was ready to fully commit. Well, we went to a Renaissance festival, and I saw one, and I just knew I would never see another one like it. As it turned out, the craftsman only made a certain number of them."

When I was getting started in the Craft and it was very important to me to have the "right" tools, I spent more money than I should have for a flat stone with a star carved into it. In retrospect, I could have made this myself and saved a few bucks. If you do want to buy your pentacle ready-made, you can get them at most Pagan shops and at a few New Age ones. There are also brass and copper pentacles with all sorts of symbols etched into them. If these symbols don't mean anything to you, don't waste your money. A rock you find in the woods will serve you just as well. If you like pretty things, keep looking till you find a pentacle that is both beautiful and meaningful to you. Don't waste your time with arcane and mysterious scribblings. There is no power in it if you don't understand it.

People treat their magical tools with varying degrees of reverence. Some believe that they should be kept separate from your other stuff and used only for magical work, and that if they are treated like ordinary objects, they will become just that.

There are others, sometimes called "kitchen Witches," who don't choose to separate the magical from the mundane, and who figure that the more an object is used, the more sacred it will be. If you live in a house where privacy is an issue, you may want to consider adopting the second attitude. If you keep your tools "sacred," that may translate to "hidden," and it's just one more thing to worry about. However, if necessary, you can always let your family think you need the glass and the kitchen knife for a snack in your room.

There are also a few tools, sometimes called "secondary tools," that are just good to have around. Various traditions incorporate some or all of them into their rituals. You, of course, can choose to use whichever ones you want, for whatever purposes you want. They can include:

- A white-handled knife, used for physical cutting (if you don't use your athame for such)
- Incense burner (one that uses charcoal and burns powder incense, and one for stick incense)
- A couple of small bowls for salt and water
- A scrying mirror (generally painted black; some books will explain how to make them, or they can be bought)
- Candles and candleholders
- A staff (basically a walking stick, it can be very ornate; sometimes used for casting circles and other energy work)
- Divination tools such as tarot cards and runes
- Jewelry and clothing for ritual and magical wear

Many of these tools can be improvised. To hold things like salt, water, and powder incense I often use shot glasses. A staff can be a large tree branch, and so on.

There are also a few things that aren't really tools at all but are very useful in ritual: a pretty cloth that will make any surface look like an altar, a candle-snuffer, a big box of kitchen matches, a flashlight (for outdoor work), a bell (nice for creating sacred space), and, last but not least, big colored votive candles to mark the four elements around the perimeter of the circle. You can find these in many urban supermarkets (often in the Hispanic specialty aisles), as well as in most occult and New Age shops.

If you want to use candles, matches, and incense in your rituals (who doesn't?), please follow some commonsense safety precautions. Never leave anything burning unattended for any length of time. Even those safe-looking seven-day votives can tip over, or the flame can catch the corner of a curtain hanging just above. It is not absolutely essential to the success of a spell that a candle burn down all the way, all at once. If you have to put a flame out, simply snuff it out and imagine yourself shutting down the spell temporarily. When you light it again, it comes back. No magic is worth putting your home and family at risk.

How to Treat Your Tools

Unless you're a kitchen Witch, it is essential to cleanse and dedicate your tools. Especially if you have purchased one from a shop or another person, it will contain all sorts of stray energy; from the person who crafted it, from the store where it was on sale, from all the hands that touched it before yours. Even if you made the tool yourself and you know its energy is pure, you should still cleanse and dedicate it before you use it. A screwdriver doesn't really care how you feel about it, but psychic tools need psychic care.

Bear in mind that tools tend to have personalities of their own. They can't perform magic without you, but they can definitely decide whether or not they like you. All things have consciousness, from the stick in the woods to the $300-handcrafted crystal wand. Every one must be respected.

When you're trying to decide whether a tool is right for you, try asking it silently how it feels about you and the idea of working together. You will sense either an enthusiastic yes!, a no!, or perhaps plain silence. If the answer is no, put it down and forget about it. Were you to buy it, it would not work for you. Yes! is a clear signal to go ahead. Silence means only that the tool is neutral, and you can claim it for your use when you cleanse it and dedicate it.

One major drawback to this method: Extremely expensive tools may shout "YES!" to you. But, you know, this may not be the actual voice of the tool. And sometimes you just have to say, "Thanks, but not right now." If price is a problem, overcome the urge to haggle. It seems to be a very, very old rule that you must never dispute the price of an object to be dedicated for magical use. To do so is disrespectful. (As far as I know, though, payment plans are okay.)

 EXERCISE: Cleansing and Dedicating a Tool

There are many, many ways to cleanse and dedicate a new tool. Feel free to improve upon my methods.

Here are a few ways to get rid of stray energy in a new tool, each corresponding to an element. You won't need to do more than one of these things unless your tool was previously owned by Jack the Ripper, or for some other reason possesses a lot of negative energy.

1. Burial. The Earth is the great recycler, and will effectively absorb anything negative that might be lurking in an object. To protect your tool, seal it in plastic. You might want to leave it underground for a few days. Just don't forget where you put it! One quick way of using this method for athames is to simply plunge the blade into the ground (check for rocks first!) and imagine all the old energy going down through the blade and into the dark earth.

2. Immersion in saltwater. Salt is a purifying material, and water is great for cleansing. The ocean, tears, and a large part of our blood are saltwater, and so it is sacred to the Goddess. Just be cautious, because saltwater is such a great purifier that it may go overboard and corrode your tool. When in doubt, instead of an overnight soak, give it a quick dip.

3. Soaking in sunlight. This is the most gentle method I know of, and it works just fine. Choose a sun-filled windowsill and leave the tool there for a few days. The sun will burn away most of the old energy and the wind blows away the rest. Just being under the sky helps things return magically to a purer state. You can test this by spending a day outdoors yourself.

4. Passing through flame. You know from playing with candle flames (and who hasn't?) that if you pass your finger through the flame fast enough, you'll barely feel the heat. The same technique can be used to cleanse most tools; just be careful with the wooden ones. If metal or stone tools blacken, the carbon can be easily wiped off. Like salt, fire is naturally purifying.

So how long does it take to cleanse a tool? I wish I could tell you, "three full moons," or something equally mystical. But the fact is, it's clean when you decide it's clean. So it may take one plunge in the earth, or it may take a week in saltwater. Hold the tool in your hands and ask yourself if it's clean. Or better yet, ask *it* if it's clean.

When your tool is cleansed, the next step is to consecrate it for your use. You can make up your own ritual, of course—but here is a simple way to do it:

Set up sacred space for yourself and cast a protective circle of energy (see Ritual chapter for more) if you like. On your altar, you will need a candle and matches, incense, a bowl of water, and a bowl of salt. Light the candle and the incense. Pass your tool through the incense smoke, saying, "I bless and consecrate you with the element of air, to be my athame (wand, etc.), to aid me in magic and to serve the Gods. So mote it be." ("Mote" is an old-fashioned English word for "must." This phrase is equivalent to "amen" in Wicca—and is a good way to cement a spell or blessing.) Do this with each of the other three elements, fire, water, and earth. Make up different words if you want. The point is to bless your tool four times over, repeating the words in order to form a strong connection between you and your tool.

Then hold it up and say, "I bless and consecrate you with the love of the Lord and Lady, that our purpose will be true and we will work for the good of all. So mote it be."

Hold your tool to your heart and feel the connection you have created. Sit and meditate for a while and see what comes to you. Afterward, write down any impressions you get in your journal.

If you have a set of your own magical tools, you will need to decide whether it's okay for other people to handle them. Some will never let another person handle their tools, some will allow only trusted friends to have that privilege. When someone touches an object, his energy affects and changes the energy of the object. And if these tools are meant to be used by only you, you may want to have only your own energy there.

KERRI: "I treat my tools with a lot of reverence and respect. Unless I hand them to another practitioner to use, they're off-limits to everyone but myself."

A rather sophisticated altar, set up for a working circle
at a friend's apartment. That lump is actually a
beautiful Goddess statue.

On the other hand, some people will let just about anyone hold
their tools, figuring that the dedication they did was complete
enough that no amount of handling by others could disrupt it. The
only rule on this subject is this: If you don't want just anyone
touching your tools, don't leave them sitting out in the open. No
matter how obvious you make your altar, people won't recognize
it as such. Even if they do, they probably won't understand the
idea of a sacred object. So if the idea of your great-aunt Josie picking up your wand and saying, "Oh, how *pretty*," bothers you, keep
your tools out of sight.

Don't worry about having magical tools right away. They will
come to you when the time is right. You don't really need any of
them to work magic. In the following section on ritual form, most
of the steps in ritual don't require any tools other than things you
ordinarily have around the house. You might want to buy some
candles, but that's about it. Your mind and your will are your only
true tools, anyway. Learn to use those first, and the rest will
follow.

The Ritual Altar

The ritual altar serves a dual purpose: It's a place to keep your ritual tools and materials handy, and it servers as a visual focus for your magical work. So any tools you will be using should be placed on the altar, and the colors, decorations, and candles all need to be appropriate to the ritual you're doing as well as visually appealing. Unsightly but necessary components, such as that box of matches from the bar down the street, or grape juice bottle, can go underneath or beside the altar.

If you have a permanent altar in your home already, you can change or add to it according to the purposes of your ritual. But if you're working somewhere else, or don't want to mess with your current altar, you can make a temporary ritual altar very easily. Any flat, firm surface—a scarf on the floor, a desk or table top, a chest, a box, or a chair—will do for a base. When outdoors, tree stumps and big flat rocks also work well.

Some people say the altar always goes in the east, or in the center of the circle. If a particular location is meaningful for you, by all means put your altar there. But more important, put it somewhere you will be able to see it easily, where you'll be able to reach the things you need to reach, and where you won't trip over it. Simple enough?

It is traditional to cover the altar with a cloth, the color of which is symbolic of the occasion. (It also makes a milk crate look much more mystical.) You don't have access to large swatches of fabric? Try long skirts, several scarves, tablecloths—even oversized T-shirts will do, if the surface is small enough.

Because candles drip, sparks fly, and wine stains, don't use any piece of material or clothing to which you are very attached. You do not have to cover the altar with a cloth. If you are using a nice polished wood table or a tree stump, you might want to leave it bare. One of the most beautiful altars I have ever seen was a round table with a clear glass surface.

You will also probably want to have at least one candle on the altar. I prefer to use a few. Many Witches like to do ritual in semi-darkness, which, as we all know, is mystical and mysterious. But it is not mystical to trip over things or to have to squint to read your invocation. I have three candles on the altar: two tapers for the God and Goddess, and one votive, which I call the "Source" candle. Since both God and Goddess emanate from the same Source, it seems to make sense. The Source candle gets lit first, even before the circle is cast, so that I can see what I'm doing. Then, when I do my invocations, I use that flame to light all the others. This centers the circle.

Many people like to have some representation of the God and Goddess on the altar. It's pretty easy to buy small statues of "popular" Gods like Pan and Aphrodite, or of the Hindu deities. You might also want to use small paintings, drawings, or sculptures you make yourself. The symbols can be anything that brings to mind the qualities of the God and Goddess. The coven I trained with used a spiral seashell for the Goddess and the breastbone of a chicken for the God (it looks like horns). On my permanent altar I have a perfectly round stone for the Goddess and a small horn for the God.

Use of statues in worship can be very effective. It puts the idea of an abstract concept into a concrete and recognizable package. In sacred space, if you treat the statue with the same respect and reverence you would show the Goddess herself, it will be an effective symbol.

You should also place some items on your altar that are relevant to the ritual you're doing. If it's a spring celebration, get some flowers or green leaves. If it's a magical working for another person, have his photograph there. One Yule we covered the floor around the altar with fake cotton snow. Have fun with it!

✂ EXERCISE: Creating a Ritual Altar

> Make a list of the things you would put on an altar for a basic full-moon ritual. Use some of the things I've listed as well as your own ideas about what should be there. Remember to include a symbol of the moon to act as a focus for the ritual. Set up the altar as if you were going to go ahead and do the ritual. Make it beautiful. Now do what you like; light the candles, burn the incense, or just sit and look at it, meditating on the symbols you have gathered together. Write about it in your journal.

Tools have an important place in most people's magical lives, but let me stress again that none of them are necessary. When I first started doing ritual, my altar had four items on it: a candle for fire, a cup for water, a stick of incense for air, and a small potted plant for earth. It worked just fine. Often, when I do rituals outdoors, I leave out the tools completely. After all, why focus on symbols of the elements when the elements themselves surround you? Just remember, the saw doesn't cut the wood by itself. And you cannot have too little on your altar, but can definitely have too much.

> BLAIR: "I don't use tools and altars that much. I believe in magic, I believe in energy, I *use* energy. But I've never gotten to the point where I think I need tools to focus a faith that I personally have. One reason I go skyclad is because I don't want to be at all false. . . . I look at even a wand or a crafted tool as being something—even if it's subconsciously—that might be a . . . mask. A lot of people have wands that they find or craft, but my hands are enough of a focusing tool for the Gods that it's not necessary to pick up something else, to disturb something else, to give praise."

It can be fun to collect pretty Pagan toys. Most Wiccans have at least one set of magical tools, and many more have sacred objects all over their homes. But remember that your tools should act as an extension of *you*. The tool you make yourself will almost always be more powerful than one you buy.

By the way, you don't have to be doing a whole ritual just to use your tools. Magic is not restricted to a ritual context. If you're feeling powerless, pick up your athame. If you're trying to conceive a child, put that phallic wand next to your bed. Ground with your pentacle. Tools are meant to be used!

CHAPTER SEVEN

Ritual

MISHA: "Let's say I lived under this wonderful fig tree, and figs fell from the tree and I ate them, and when it rained the fig tree kept me dry . . . and when it was too sunny the fig tree would protect me from the sun. And so what would I do? I might decide that this fig tree was a wonderful thing and I would have rituals to give thanks to it for what it gave me. And on some level I would hope that it was aware of the rituals.

"We know the Earth is alive, that it nurtures life from its own body. If I go up on a hillside and perform rituals and participate in a ritual of thanks to the Earth Goddess, I don't know that she has a consciousness. I believe she has an awareness. But that's where knowledge ends and belief begins."

Witches define ritual as a sacred symbolic act. We use props, words, and gestures to affect our deeper selves and the world around us. Instead of scripted rituals, this chapter includes all the information you need to create them yourself—which is far more meaningful and effective than parroting someone else's words.

Almost any act, not just religious ceremony, can be made sacred. The intent is what makes the difference. You can go to Catholic mass and participate in Holy Communion, but if your mind is elsewhere, it will mean nothing. You can also make your morning shower into a ritual of cleansing and transformation with the right intent. Effective ritual is not a bunch of gestures someone performs just to please their Gods, religious leaders, family, or government. The participant must be affected in some positive and lasting way.

> OBSIDIANA: "A lot of [bad rituals] are just mechanical. Everything is by rote, and there's no emotion behind it. Because there are so many props and everything else, they look impressive. But there's nothing behind it. It's kind of like a very shallow play. And if you're so hung up on pronouncing every word correctly and not missing this person's name or that Deity's name, you lose it."

You can create a ritual for any reason, but rituals generally fall into two categories. First, they can be *celebratory*, which includes all the holidays and full moons as well as rites of passage, such as a birth. The ritual is a way for you to acknowledge the event or change, celebrate it, and let yourself be affected by that change. *Ritual magic*, on the other hand, is very different, and requires a much more active role. Those doing the ritual create a set of images, words, and movements to help focus their will and energy toward achieving their goal. Many rituals incorporate elements of both celebration and magic.

It is not difficult to write and perform a ritual. There are no rules, so it is impossible to do it "wrong." The ritual may turn out to be unsuccessful, but that's how we learn. If you're practicing alone, there will be no one there but you and the Gods. And they have a sense of humor.

> LORRIE: "One really great circle is one I did on my back deck on Mabon with my husband and brother-in-law. There was a

full moon and I knew they were a little nervous, but when I invoked the Goddess after casting the circle, these large cow bells I had hanging on the pine tree next to the deck began to ring. There was not even a breeze and no one standing near them. I thought my brother-in-law was going to jump out of his skin, so I laughed and grabbed both him and my husband by the arms and said, 'It's okay, she doesn't bite.' We all laughed and continued the rite. He still tells people about that."

OBSIDIANA: "At some of the best circles, where I really had fun, we would be silly and at ease and relaxed, and would just have a good time. The first circle we did together was on Yule. We were all sitting cross-legged on the floor, and Barbara was blessing a tray of cookies, and she holds the cookies up, and the cookies are dropping off in her lap, and she says, 'And don't forget the ones that fell in my lap!' I've been to circles where if that happened, everyone would have been like, 'GASP!' I'm much more comfortable in a circle where there's a free exchange of energy between us. Where you can laugh."

Whether you're doing a healing spell for a friend or performing a sabbat ritual, the basic outline is the same. It's used because it works, not because anyone tells us to do it this way. Within that outline, there is a lot of room for improvisation. Casting a circle is an important step, for instance, but there are any number of ways to cast a circle, ranging from the simple few seconds of visualization to a complex and intricate ritual casting that involves several tools, elaborate gestures, scripted words, and at least three trips around the circle. You will have to decide how to craft each step, considering your own tastes, the nature of the occasion, and the other people present.

The materials recommended for the ritual steps below include: three candles for the altar (God, Goddess, and Source), four candles for the elements, matches, a full chalice, an athame, and some kind of cakes or cookies. You will also need any materials you will be using in the center of the ritual. Use more or less, as you wish. Everything should be in the area before you start.

The prelude to ritual should include a few moments of silent meditation, grounding, deep breathing, and focusing on your purpose. It makes the transition into sacred space a lot easier, and it makes the ritual more productive because you are more fully "there."

Then, most Wiccan ritual includes the following steps: You establish sacred space, call on the Gods/powers to witness and help, declare your intent, and perform some kind of symbolic act that will be the central focus of the ritual. Then you give thanks, have a small feast, and go back to "regular" space. Here are the steps of Wiccan ritual in more detail.

The Opening

Creating sacred space. This is the moment when you begin to transform your home into your temple. You might want to start with a magical cleansing of the space, with saltwater or incense. And then try turning off the lights and lighting a candle, ringing a bell, closing the door, or putting on a certain kind of music. Your goal is to slow down, become aware, feel the presence of Divinity within and around you, and to surround yourself with a feeling of safety and serenity. This sets the stage for the magical work. When I light the Source candle on my altar, that is when I am in sacred space.

> VICTORIA: "In [massage] class, I was working on a friend who wanted to have some emotional release, but didn't feel comfortable in front of all the other people around. So I told my friend, 'Imagine sacred space around us, and nothing that you are comfortable letting out will be let out, and nothing distracting will be let in.' I said, 'How do you feel?' and he said, 'Whoa, I feel that,' and our work together flowed better. So now when I'm working with someone, I don't necessarily cast a formal circle, but I do create a sacred space around us of complete safety and unconditional love. That's part of our training, to surround someone with unconditional love."

Casting the circle. Here, you will create, through your force of will, a protective magical enclosure inside of which you will do your magic. The circle will keep any energy you raise from leaking away, and it will protect you from any unwanted influences. The circle also creates a space that is neither physical nor spiritual. It touches on all the worlds, but is confined to none.

It is possible to cast a circle through simple visualization, but if you are just beginning, it will be easier if you actually go through the movements. Take a moment to focus yourself through a couple of deep breaths. Go to the wall (or the edge of where you want your circle to be) and hold out your hand (or wand, or athame). Draw energy up from the soles of your feet and push it out through your fingers to form the circle and walk slowly around the room, clockwise. Imagine the energy forming not a ring, but a three-dimensional enclosure, around you and your sacred space. For practicality's sake, most people tend to imagine the circle stretching out to the walls, rather than being a perfect sphere.

While you're doing this, you can focus on any images that will help you. Sometimes, depending on the nature of the ritual, I will see the circle as a warm, protective blanket that I am spreading over the room. Other times it's a sparkling, cascading rainbow of colors. It may help if you say something as you do it, such as "I cast this circle in love and trust, to protect me, and transport me to the realms of the Gods. So mote it be." You might also want to throw in something about the reason for the ritual. There are more and less formal castings than this—you can find them in other books, or you can write your own.

Some people use salt, sand, stones, or paint to actually mark out the circle on the floor. This really isn't necessary and sometimes might be just plain inconvenient. To this day, I don't know what I was thinking when, at age sixteen, I asked my mother if I could paint a permanent circle on the wood floor of my room! You also don't want to have to vacuum up a lovely mess of sand. Simple visualization is enough. Outdoors, you can be more elaborate. Just make sure to clean up afterward.

After you cast the circle, you should consider it a real structure, and therefore you should not walk through it. First, it weakens the circle. Especially if there are other people in circle with you, it won't feel good to them. It's like letting a cold wind into a warm room. And second, remember that the purpose of ritual is to affect your unconscious mind through the use of symbolism. If you treat the circle as something real, its effects will be stronger in your own mind. If you treat it carelessly, as if it isn't really there, it won't do the work it's supposed to do.

If you must leave circle, you will need to cut a gateway to step through without disturbing the rest of the circle. I have been to enough rituals with people who have crying babies, small bladders, or faulty memories to know that "gating out" is perfectly fine. Some people trace an entire doorway in the circle, walk through it, and then close the doorway. I just use my hands to part the circle like a pair of curtains, walk through, and close the curtains behind me. Use any method you want; just make sure you stay mindful and respectful of the circle. Try not to gate out too often; doing so will weaken the circle somewhat.

Calling the quarters. Here you are going to be aligning yourself with the energies of the elements, which sounds a lot fancier than it actually is. You remember that each element has a unique energy, and that you contain all five. You contain air because you have an intellect, fire because you have a will, water because you have emotions, and earth because you have a physical body. You contain spirit because you are a magical being with the spark of Deity within you.

When you align yourself with an element, you are simultaneously bringing it out from within you and calling it to you from the spirit realm. As you call each element, face the direction associated with it: east, air; south, fire; west, water; and north, earth.

I was taught to start in the east, since that is where the sun rises. (Some start in the north, traditionally the home of the Gods.) Face east, open your arms, or salute with your athame, and say something to call the spirit of air to you. At the least, you should speak or think some kind of welcoming, such as "Spirits of the east, powers of air, be with me in my circle tonight. Blessed be and welcome." Blow a kiss if you like, or salute with your athame. You may also light a candle corresponding to that element. But remember, you are not just speaking words and moving your arms around, you are doing magical work. You are aligning yourself with the element. So you will need to include some imagery that means "air" to you. Don't just recite a list of correspondences; use image you can relate to. A balloon may be a more effective image for you than an eagle. Imagine yourself joining with that element; become the balloon, or feel a breeze blowing over your feathers as you fly.

If you're doing ritual outdoors, calling the elements is easy. An actual breeze will blow over your skin, the hot sun will warm you, and so forth. You can focus on these sensations to bring the element to you. But if you're indoors, you need to focus on strong images that will override your physical isolation from the actual elements. One great technique that I use in group work is to ask people to call out anything they personally associate with the element we're calling on. I have gotten a lot of interesting responses: earth was brown eyeliner, water was a toilet flushing, and so forth. But amid the giggles, it worked! If you're not comfortable with "off the cuff" ritual, meditate on each of the elements beforehand, and write down some images that are meaningful to you, that you can read during the ritual.

Beware of relying on a script, however. Group rituals require a fairly detailed plan to keep everyone together and focused, but every second that you read from a piece of paper, you will be separated from your will and the purpose of the ritual. It is very difficult, if not impossible, to read a line and visualize your magical intent at the same time. If you want to use some pretty invocations or poetry, try to memorize them, or at least be very familiar with the words.

The time to connect with that energy within you and within all things, the source of all the other elements, the power of life itself, is when you call on the element of "spirit," or "center." Take a few deep breaths and maybe cross your arms over your chest as you say your invocation. This will reinforce your place in the circle, among the other elements, aligned with them and perfectly balanced between them, at the center.

JAKE: "When I lived in New Jersey, all our rituals would be in other people's places, where I was always a participant and never had the opportunity to take the reins and write a ritual, or to really understand what goes into making one. But now that I live on my own, in Arizona, and have a new group of

Pagan friends, I've become the ritual writer and the hostess. The rituals are always in my apartment. I feel like I'm a lot more involved. It's one thing to read someone else's ritual from a piece of paper, but it's another thing to be the author of the words."

Calling on the God and Goddess. Again, as with the elements, the God and Goddess are already present. But you are going to be bringing them out from within you, and making yourself aware of their existence outside of yourself. It is a *welcoming*, not a summoning.

There is a more intense version of this, called "drawing down the Moon," or "drawing down the Sun," in which the Witch allows himself to be totally absorbed into the Goddess or God. The ego takes a step back and the pure light of Deity shines through the person. Sometimes the God or Goddess will speak, using the person's voice. This is often difficult, as it requires some magical experience and a huge amount of trust. There's no reason anyone can't do this, but it's better to start slowly.

For now, call on the Gods in the same way as you did the elements. If you have God and Goddess candles on your altar, you can light each of them in turn. Say, "Bright Lady (or Horned One), I ask for your presence in my circle tonight. Blessed be and welcome." You can make this more elaborate. For me, the more poetic and powerful the words of the invocation are, the easier it is to do it. The following is a Goddess invocation I wrote for a group Samhain ritual when I was eighteen:

Great Mother of the night, I call upon thee. By the four winds that blow through us and lift our spirits, I call upon thee. In the pale moonlight, I call upon thee. Your face is shrouded in darkness, and we ask to know your secrets, O Mother of all souls. I call upon thee, Maiden Huntress whose footsteps echo through the quiet forest, bountiful Mother whose arms hold the stars, Crone of the hidden paths. Goddess whose essence is as immense as the Universe yet dwells within our hearts, I call upon thee. By the air that is your breath, the fire that is your passion, the waters that are your womb, and the earth that is your body, I call upon thee, and bid thee blessed be, and welcome.

Note that I used a lot of seasonal images: night, moon, quiet, stars, echo, pale, secrets—all of these are appropriate for Samhain. If the ritual had been for Beltane, there would have been a lot of images of sunlight, flowers, warmth, and laughter. To make your invocations really effective, don't simply call on a generic "God and Goddess," call on the aspects of them that you will want to have there for the ritual.

You don't have to get a dictionary of mythology and memorize the names of all the various Gods of the world. The names are just a convenient way for people to categorize things. If you call on Athena, or just simply say "Goddess of Wisdom," the effect will be the same.

Still, you might like to do some research, because some of the God and Goddess names of the world are beautiful and exotic, and therefore fun to use in ritual (the Aztec Storm Goddess Chalchihuitlicue, for instance). But if you don't know what they mean, and if you can't pronounce them, they will be useless. I once attended a large group ritual that relied heavily on an elaborate script. The priestess who had written the lines was obviously well-versed in mythology, and she assumed that her fellow Witches would be as well. Those who volunteered to assist in the ritual were faced with the task of reading out loud such names as Coatlicue, Mictanteot, Ereshkigal, Julunggul, and Urcaguary. The long pauses and nervous giggling did somewhat interfere with the effectiveness of the ritual, especially since it was meant to be solemn. So if you just say "Dark Lady" instead of "Hecate Epitymbidia," you will probably have better luck. (No, I don't know how to pronounce that one either.)

The Middle

The focus of the ritual. You have set up your sacred circle and called on the elements and the Gods to help you along. Now what? Many people put so much energy into their setup that the main part of the ritual becomes an afterthought. Don't let that happen to you! If you must skimp on something, make the setup and take-down simple, and save the powerful stuff for the center.

For both celebratory and magical rituals, you can use one or more of the following:

- Power-raising
- Magical drama
- Symbolic acts (egg decorating on Ostara, jumping the broom in a handfasting (wedding), making a talisman for a spell, and so on)
- Meditation/trancework
- Singing/chanting
- Traditional/magical games (many kissing games apply)
- Dancing (spiral dance, maypole dance)
- Playing musical instruments (drums are popular)
- Storytelling

Of course, you can combine a few of these, like dancing, drumming, and chanting, or music and symbolic acts, or drama and meditation—the possibilities are endless. Working solitary will limit your choices somewhat: The center of your ritual will probably have to be a little quieter and more focused on meditation. But you can do anything you want; it's your show.

> JAKE: "I always like to have some cool creative group project. Once, in the middle of the ritual, we all sat down around a small table, and I took a big piece of paper and we all just painted a picture. And it wasn't 'of' anything, you would just kind of draw whatever you wanted to and it would become a part of what the other guy was drawing. The point of the thing was all things becoming one."

If you are planning a ritual for one of the sabbats, your goal is to become connected to the season. Read up on that sabbat, meditate for a while on its particular meaning, and try to come up with a way to immerse yourself in that meaning.

One of my favorite seasonal rituals is one I did for Imbolc when I was in college. After we had set up the circle, we took a little snow that we had saved from that winter and put it into a butter warmer. We placed a candle underneath it, which became symbolic of the sun melting away the winter cold. As the snow melted, I told the myth of Persephone's springtime journey from the underworld into the arms of her mother, Demeter, the Grain Goddess. When the snow had all melted and my story was over, we poured the water into a vase of white flowers.

My friend said, "Now I ask you all to visualize new growth—be it plants budding, as in the growth of the Earth, or else your own personal growth, which is equally important. Empower these flowers with that energy. We call upon the God and Goddess in each of us, that they may aid us in our work."

We started a low chant and quietly channeled the energy we raised into the flowers. Then everyone was given a flower to take home, wet from the melted snow, and filled with positive energy.

The "main part" of your ritual need not always include a power-raising, but that is a nice way to structure it. That way, the ritual will have a very clear buildup, a peak, and a cooldown. Whatever you do, the ritual should reflect the nature of the occasion. Beltane, for instance, is a good time for a rowdy, silly maypole dance that everyone will screw up, and then they can collapse, laughing hysterically (or, if you're working solitary, something similarly lighthearted). You wouldn't want to do that at Yule. Your wintertime ritual should contain elements of the serene, the barren. Instead of a rowdy dance-and-drum session, why not try a meditation or a quiet, intense chant?

If you're doing ritual with others, you may want to act out some kind of short drama, with the characters either deities or elements of Nature. Drama can be a very powerful medium to get a message across. When the ancient Greeks wrote those plays our teachers forced us to read in school, they were not meant to be the subjects of term papers, but rather intense emotional experiences! Those watching the drama will be strongly affected; staring into the face of a God or Goddess is a lot more powerful than just hearing a pretty invocation. Those acting out the parts will be strongly affected as well, because they are, in a sense, "becoming" the characters.

There are two possible purposes for the ritual in a rite-of-passage ceremony. You might want to simply mark and celebrate a change of life. For example, you don't have to attend your graduation to get your diploma; it's a formality that you may want to participate in for the sentimental value. However, the ceremony may also have magical elements to it, either to help the passage along or to complement it. For instance, in a Wiccaning (child blessing), the participants may ask the Gods for their blessing of the baby, and may also do protection spells. In a divorce, or handparting ceremony, there may be a symbolic "parting of the ways" and also a working to strengthen the two people in their new separate paths. Ideally, a rite-of-passage ritual should be *both* a celebration of a passage and a magical "push" to help the passage along.

Our society recognizes certain passages with a lot of pageantry, such as weddings and funerals. But others that are just as important, such as someone's first menstruation, are completely ignored. Most tribal cultures (Judaism included) have elaborate rituals that declare someone to be "officially" an adult. But other than going out to register with Selective Service, or registering to vote, for most of us our eighteenth birthday marks only another year gone. Lots of passages deserve recognition: taking the SAT's, getting your driver's license, losing your virginity, starting your first job, getting (or losing) your first boyfriend or girlfriend—any life-changing event. Maybe you need to help yourself through a tough time, or to celebrate having just come through one. Any of these are great reasons for a rite-of-passage ritual.

For simplicity's sake, we'll assume the ritual is going to be by yourself, for yourself. (It's easier to revise up than down in size) Sit and meditate on your purpose. Let's say you are about to turn thirty tomorrow. You might want to put on some music that makes you feel very confident and strong. Take a look through a photo album of your first thirty years. Give yourself a private feast of your favorite foods. Make a list of all the things of your childhood and young adulthood that you are glad to put behind you, and destroy the list. Make a list of all the things you are going to be and accomplish in the future, and say them out loud or meditate on them. Look at yourself in the mirror and tell yourself that you are an adult, you are beautiful, you are powerful. This is a celebration of how far you have come.

In order to put together the central part of a ritual done for spellwork, you should first meditate on the purpose, and then devise a way to best symbolize that purpose. The only difference here is that you will have a very definite goal, and directed intent. You want to bring love into your life. You want to get over your cold. You want a better job. Remember that in order to work an effective spell it helps to have a physical focus. Also, as in any ritual work, it is very important that you are grounded and centered beforehand.

The rest is simple. The spell will be the center of your ritual. You need not always do a whole ritual for the purposes of spellwork; if the spell is very short and simple, it would be silly to go to all that trouble. But you should at least cast a circle beforehand. If the spell is for something really challenging—like healing a friend's cancer—you might find that an elaborate setup makes you put more of yourself into your working. Think about the difference between a meal served on fine china and one on paper plates. The disposables will do, in a pinch, but doesn't the beautiful setting make you work just a bit harder on the preparation?

Cakes and ale. Especially if you've been doing any challenging magical work, you will be hungry by now. That is the practical reason for this step.

As for the *symbolic* meaning of eating blessed food in a ritual setting, I could write an entire book on that. You are probably familiar with the Christian ritual of communion. That is one of many versions of the same idea: that by eating and drinking, we are taking God/dess into our bodies and thus becoming holy ourselves. Jesus is a more recent incarnation of the dying and reborn vegetation God. We plant seeds, which grow into plants. We cut the plants down, and we are fed through their death. Then they are reborn, either through seeds left over, or from their old roots in the earth. And the cycle begins all over again. So by eating and drinking, we are participating in the cycle of life and death.

No, it doesn't have to be literally "cakes and ale." You might have some kind of cake, cookies, or bread, accompanied by wine or fruit juice. (Potato chips and ginger ale will do, if that's all there is.) If you have the time, make the food symbolic of the season, since it should represent the bounty of the Earth. For instance, how about sugar cookies and eggnog at Yule? Or wholegrain bread and apple cider at Mabon?

Even though "ale" is traditional, alcohol and magic don't really mix very well. A glass of wine might make you relaxed and make you *feel* more magical, but it really makes you more out of touch and lessens your control. For this reason—and because many people can't or won't drink—99 percent of the open rituals I've attended have been alcohol-free. If you choose to include it, do so in moderation.

Have your chalice filled with juice or wine and on the altar before you start your setup. (If you're working with others, keep the bottle within easy reach—you will need to refill it.) The bread or cakes can be put on a pretty plate, or in a basket—anything that you like the looks of, and that is seasonally appropriate. If there's no room for the plate on the altar, it can go underneath, or next to it.

First you will be doing the "wine blessing," or Great Rite in Token. Here, the athame is inserted into the chalice, to represent the union of complimentary opposites—specifically, in this case, the God and the Goddess.

The Great Rite in Truth is done when the High Priest draws down the Sun, and the High Priestess the Moon, and then they make love using their bodies as channels for the union of the two energies. Because many people do ritual alone, and because not everyone you circle with will be someone you want to make love with, and, because even if you *do* want to make love to that person, you may not want to do it in front of your coven—the Great Rite in Token was invented. The Great Rite in Truth is a transformative, powerful working, and something that many Witches never get to experience. It requires not only magical experience, but love and trust between the two people involved, as well as agreement of your intent and a good magical partnership.

Done with the proper concentration and intent, the Rite in Token can be the same kind of energy exchange as the Rite in

Truth, but on a smaller scale. The ritual purpose is twofold: to provide a focus for worship, and to bless the drink that you will be sharing. If you are alone, you can hold the chalice in one hand and the athame in the other, and lower the athame into the chalice. As you do this, imagine the God's energy extending down one arm and the Goddess's down the other, and the two energies blending within the cup. You contain them both within yourself, so there is no reason you cannot do this alone. (For the Great Rite in Truth, I think you'll need a partner.)

As you bring the cup and athame together, you might want to say a few words. When two people do the blessing, they take turns speaking. In one version, the person holding the athame says, "As the athame is to the lover," and the person with the chalice returns, "So the cup is to the beloved." The athame is lowered into the chalice, and together they say, "And when joined, they become one in truth." If you're alone, just say the whole thing yourself. Or spend a few seconds in silent meditation on the image of the Joining.

Once you have done this, the drink is blessed. If you're going to refill it, make sure to keep some of the original liquid in there. That keeps the blessing in.

Now you will bless the cakes or bread. This isn't as big a deal; it's actually more of a thanksgiving than a working. The wording my old coven used was, "May the Gods bless all hands seen and unseen who have brought this bread (or these cakes) to us." There is no particular way to hold the bread that I know of; just do what feels right. You might want to stick the tip of your athame into it as you say the blessing, to infuse it with magic.

One Lughnassadh, my group was doing a ritual in a public park. We had baked a loaf of bread in the shape of a man, to represent the dying and reborn God. I decided to make the bread blessing particularly dramatic, so I lifted my athame up high, and plunged it into the heart of the bread-man. I was deep in concentration, of course, but others told me afterward that a police officer had come walking by right at that moment of truth. That loaf of bread had been about the size and shape of a newborn baby; from a distance, the blessing must have looked a bit unnerving. Luckily, the officer figured out that it was just a loaf of bread, or we might have had to pause in our ritual for a bit of public education.

When you're working with a group, you might like to pass the cup around. As each person receives it, she says a few words—whatever comes to mind—and takes a sip. Most people offer a "libation" at this time. That means you spill a few drops on the ground as thanks to the Gods from whence it came. Indoors, you can use a "libation bowl," or simply save a bit at the end to take outside and pour on the ground. It is considered good form to offer thanks in some way. The cup goes around as many times as it's wanted.

The basket or plate with the bread follows the cup around the circle. Alone, simply take some for yourself, and offer silent or spoken thanks.

In groups, this is generally the time for sharing, talking, joking around, and generally enjoying the energy that's there. Alone, you might want to spend a few moments in meditation.

The Closing

Thanking the God and Goddess. "Dismissals" are not usually as elaborate as the invocations. They don't require as much concentration or focus, and by the time you get to the end of the circle, people are going to be a lot less focused anyway. This is mostly a matter of giving thanks for the presence of the Gods in the ritual, and also a way for you to release the energy you have raised.

Dismissals are a way of saying "goodnight and thanks for coming." (Any ideas you may have of calling on energies to "do one's bidding" do not belong in Wicca. The Gods often find ways to cut people with ideas like that down to size.) When you dismiss the God and Goddess, you are moving your consciousness out of the deep level of ritual and back into a more physical level.

You might want to say something like, "Horned One (or Bright Lady), your presence has blessed us. Before you return to your lovely realm, we bid you hail and farewell." Blow or snuff out the candles that represent the God and Goddess.

Thanking the elements. Some people believe that you should do everything clockwise (deosil) in circle, since counterclockwise (widdershins) is considered "negative" movement. I prefer to thank the elements in reverse order, starting with north and going counterclockwise west, then south, and ending with east. Whatever order you use, you'll salute each direction and say, "I [we] give thanks to the element of Earth for your presence in my [our] circle tonight. Hail and farewell." Blow or snuff out the candles that represent the elements as you dismiss them.

Taking down the circle. Again, do this widdershins if that makes sense to you. You can use your athame or wand, your hand, or use this pretty and effective method I learned in my old coven: Take the Source candle from the altar, and as you walk around the perimeter of the circle, say, "Fire seal the circle 'round, let it fade beneath the ground. Let all things be as they were since the beginning of time." Repeat this if you like. As you walk around, imagine the energy of the circle falling back to the Earth, sinking in like water to soil, being reclaimed by the Mother. You can also take some of that energy back into yourself for healing. Just make sure to give thanks to the Earth from which it came.

Then blow out the candle. If you're in a group, say, "The circle is open, but never broken. Merry meet, and merry part, and merry meet again!" (or write your own conclusion) If alone, just quietly bring your consciousness back to your regular space. I've always found that turning on an electric light helps bring me back.

And then you are done! It is generally a good rule to wait until the next day to analyze or discuss any rituals you do. They need time to sink in.

KAREN: "The more ceremonially oriented people are, the more rigid they are in their thinking. That's not to say that people involved in ceremonial magic aren't mining a very rich vein in spirituality, just that they tend to be people who enjoy structure. I enjoy a certain amount of structure, and it's great to have a good solid structural part when you're learning, but as time goes by . . . in my case I've found that having sort of internalized a lot of the structures, I'm kind of freed up to play with it. Really, what the structures of the traditions are, more than anything it's like a common language, a language of symbols, so that people will have an idea of what they're doing when they're in a group. It's kind of like having a frame, and then you hang everything else around it. You have a language and you can say anything within that language. Structure is a useful reference."

You can also be a Witch without ever doing a ritual. The Craft is a philosophy and a way of life, not a set of tasks. If you do decide to try rituals, remember a few things:

1. You are expected to make mistakes. The Gods have a sense of humor; don't lose yours.
2. Don't ever make the ritual more important than the intent behind it.
3. Do ritual because you want to, not because you think you have to.
4. Do your research and ask questions. Do not ever do anything in ritual that you do not understand. You will be wasting your time.
5. If it doesn't feel right, don't do it!

CHAPTER EIGHT

The Other Side: Expanding Your Awareness

JAKE: "Ever since I can remember, from early childhood, I've had an astounding sixth sense. I know I'm empathic, and often I can predict what other people are going to say before they say it. Maybe it's just really, really refined perception skills. I don't think there's much of a difference."

The physical world we experience is only one tiny part of the whole. Being a Witch means being able to function in other worlds as well. This can be as simple as the attention we give to the messages in our dreams, to the task of developing our psychic abilities, to undertaking the challenge of a deep trance. As a Witch you can see beyond appearances. This can be very useful, but—as do all new skills—it brings new challenges.

Many people have had some kind of psychic experience, been hypnotized, done a meditation or relaxation exercise, or tried a divination technique such as tarot cards or runes. Everyone dreams, and most people remember their dreams at least some of the time. Essentially, we all spend at least a third of our lives (when sleeping) in other worlds.

The unseen world, though somewhat familiar, is often frightening. The rules are different, the settings are weird. We can feel powerful when we discover our own psychic abilities—but can also be frightened by a nightmare. And on the other side, we are confronted with parts of ourselves we might prefer to disown— we're mean, selfish, hurtful, or "oversexed." We see our shadows.

Why not try to forget about it, then? Maybe we should just stick to the world we know and stay away from the one we don't. Maybe we're just not meant to mess around there. Maybe it's too risky, too unsafe. Maybe it's evil.

Well, if you want a comfy, safe religion, look elsewhere. Witchcraft is an initiatory path. That means we are required to stretch and test ourselves all the time. If we are not challenged, we are stagnant. The lurking shadows in our nightmares aren't evil; they're only problems waiting to be fixed. They can't be fixed without some risk. And true risk brings fear.

Whether we realize it or not, the unseen world is influencing the physical one all the time. On a personal level, our unconscious mind affects our worldview. On a larger scale, forces such as karma, cause and effect, and all sorts of magical practices are altering the world we see. The memories and spirits of our ancestors, the force of Deity—these are all hidden but real influences.

And we exist in that other world all the time, whether we choose to acknowledge it or not. We are made of more than our physical bodies and the electrical charge of neurons in our brains. We are magical, spiritual beings. The human aura can be felt, and its energy will help or harm the physical body it pervades and surrounds. When we dream, we exist in another universe, one that seems just as real as this one. Who's to say which is real and which is a dream? Why ignore one in favor of another?

For a Witch, indeed, anyone who wants to develop her sense of spirituality, it is essential to learn how to function in these other worlds and to learn how to use her other senses. It is the only way to be a fully conscious being, rather than someone who is asleep half the time, or unaware of half of her existence. Most magical skills—spellwork, ritual, trance, and divination—require a Witch to "speak the language" of the other side. In addition, journeys in meditation and dreamwork will help the individual to function better in the physical world. And when you come to know your *own* "other side," the mood swings and desires of your conscious mind won't be such a mystery anymore.

It's not hard to learn this skill. It's more a matter of remembering. Babies are born with the ability to move between both worlds because they haven't yet been taught otherwise. Children have imaginary friends—how many, do you suppose, might be visiting spirits? Even a child's game of make-believe feels so real to him, because he is experiencing an alternate world that may actually *be* real, in some sense.

Most people use their natural psychic abilities every now and then, often as an accident, because they don't believe in them and weren't consciously trying to use them. But something is at work. Your relative was in a car crash and you allowed yourself to sense it, because your help was needed. You knew the precise moment when your friend had her baby because, deep down, it was important to you to know.

You can make a conscious choice to use these abilities. If you have had a psychic experience, think back to how it happened. Did the information come as a visual image, a sound, a physical feeling? Did something distinguish it from a casual thought? How was your mood that day? If you can recreate the feeling, you can nurture that feeling and work with it, until it is under the control of your conscious mind.

If you have had psychic experiences several times, it's even better, because you will be able to map the similarities between them. Were you feeling especially relaxed at these times? Was the experience touched off by a catastrophic event? Was there a similarity between these feelings?

AUTUMN: "When my girlfriend and I started, we would work on sending different colors back and forth, and an image with the color, you know, like 'water,' and 'blue,' or 'the sun' and 'orange,' and after a while it was not a coincidence anymore, how many times we got it right, what the other person was thinking. I just think that's a really good way to start developing your psychic skills. She and I had been really good friends for a while, and we were very close, and it was easier that way. If it were someone I wasn't all that familiar with, it probably would've taken longer."

If you have never had a psychic experience, it doesn't mean you lack the ability. You just need to purposefully retune your consciousness to a different frequency. There are many good books available with exercises for developing your psychic abilities, and practice is always good. On an everyday level, though, just pay attention to those thoughts that seem to "pop" into your head—especially those that seem to come out of nowhere. You may be trying to tell yourself something.

Expanding Your Awareness

Most of us go through our day with blinders on, only noticing those things we have deemed important, and only those things we expect. When I owned a baby boa constrictor, occasionally I went on my errands with her wrapped around my wrist or around my ponytail. I didn't call attention to her at all, and as a result, 75 percent of the people I encountered simply didn't see her. I even went through an entire purchase in a store with her wrapped around my wrist, and the sales clerk never said a word. When I was done, I was curious as to whether he was deliberately trying to ignore the snake, and I pointed her out. The clerk was quite startled. This was someone with tunnel vision. He was the kind of person who is not going to hang out on the other side, because he isn't even fully aware of the one he's currently living in!

The Zen philosophy of mindfulness is the first thing you need to develop. It means being fully aware of your existence. That includes the self as well as the environment. If you are being mindful, you will be just as aware of the taste of the gum in your mouth as you will be of the sound of a bird chirping in a tree on the other side of the block. This is not a forced kind of focus, but it does require attention and a degree of discipline. It leads to a calm, but awake, sort of feeling. To achieve it means slowing down and being still and quiet a few times each day. Can you find your way around your apartment with your eyes closed? If not, you haven't been mindful of your environment.

Many Americans aren't mindful because we rarely do one thing at a time. We're all in a rush, and we all want constant stimulation. We sometimes find ourselves eating, watching TV, and reading simultaneously. While it is certainly efficient and timesaving, the problem is that we are only half-experiencing the food, the show, and the book.

✄ EXERCISE: Eat an Orange

That's all. Do absolutely nothing else. Do not allow yourself to dwell on any extraneous thought. All your attention should be on the color, texture, the weight of the fruit, the feeling of separating the peel from the fruit, the smell that hits your nose when it is opened, the act of separating the sections, the feel and the taste of the juicy fruit in your mouth. Do this exercise correctly, and you may realize that you probably haven't actually tasted anything in a long time, if ever. Try to carry that sense of mindfulness into the other things you do.

You do not have to wait until you're superaware of your existence in the physical world before you go exploring elsewhere. The two disciplines can be developed at the same time and will help each other along. To explore the other side, there are lots of safe and effective ways to get started. None of them requires any kind of commitment, and they can be taken at any pace.

Pay attention to your dreams. For many people, dreams are real journeys into another world. Think back to the more vivid dreams you have had. Were there any times when you were able to influence the outcome of a dream? Times when dreams felt more "real" than usual? What kind of imagery do you see in your dreams, over and over again, and how does that imagery surface in your conscious, waking life?

Dream books are often kept in the New Age section of book-stores, not in the psychology/self-help area, for a reason. It's the same reason that books on the Craft are located in that section, and not with other religious books. The common thread among these books is the element of magic and mystery. These subjects are *occult*, which means "hidden." Dreams, astrology, UFO's, tarot, spirit guides, and Wicca are grouped together. In all these sub-jects, that which is not seen—the mystery—is more important than appearances.

You may think that dreams are just your brain's way of having a little fun while you're asleep. Actually, they are absolutely essen-tial to your mental health. Studies have shown that people who are deprived of dreaming have trouble functioning in their daily lives and may eventually start to hallucinate.

Every being exists simultaneously on many different levels, from the mundane knowledge we need for daily life, down to our thoughts and feelings, and then down to the deepest level where dreams live. On that level, we are fully aware of ourselves, no deceptions allowed. Here, traumatic events and "dangerous" emotions we would prefer to forget are still remembered. It is so far removed from the everyday that the language is that of myth, ritual, and magic: symbols. And that's where the "shadow" lives.

The inner self, the deepest self that brings you into your dream journey, is also that part of you that is most in touch with the Divine and with magic. The battles you fight in your dreams are as real as any you'll fight in the physical world—and will probably have a greater impact on your life in the long run.

Dreamwork is an excellent way to get started in your journey to the other side, for a few reasons: First of all, you dream all the time, so it's familiar. Second, and most important, dreams incor-porate all the most difficult elements of this kind of journey: Here, your degree of control is minimal. There's no way to plan it, and therefore no way to be prepared. Also, many of these images—representing the naked truth about yourself—will be disturbing. When you have worked through a horrific nightmare and have come out stronger, little you see in trance will faze you.

So how do you make the most of your mandatory journeys over there? Before you go to sleep, take a minute or so to silently affirm a willingness to learn whatever your inner self has to show you. If you feel the need, also affirm that your are divinely protected and divinely safe. The battles *are* real, but your life won't be in peril.

While you're dreaming, try to keep an awareness of that willingness to learn in the back of your mind. it's difficult, but possible. You can achieve different degrees of "lucidity" in your dreams, ranging from the slight idea that perhaps something isn't quite right, to the full consciousness that you are currently dreaming (which is really fun, I might add). Let the dream take you where it wants to go, and try to use the experience for all it's worth. Inside the dream, try asking people and symbols who and what they represent—they may tell you!

When you wake up, pay attention to your emotions. Symbols alone will not tell you anything. There are "dream dictionaries" that promise a fill-in-the-blank kind of interpretation. A train always means one thing, a mountain means another. But, as mentioned in the magic chapter, there are very few universal symbols. If you have always had a phobia of cats and I keep one as a pet, that symbol is going to mean different things depending on which of us dreaming. If you have the discipline for it, it's great to keep a dream journal. As soon as you wake up, write down everything that happened, even bits you think are inconsequential.

You can spend as little or as much time as you want on your dreams. It may be enough just to experience them and sit with the feelings and the images for a while, or you might want to write everything down and then record some later thoughts as well. It is important to give your dreams *some* attention. They're happening for a reason: You are trying to send yourself a message. Once you become willing to hear what you have to say, then your magic will become much more effective.

Meditate. Meditation is a discipline that has been practiced for thousands of years, so there must be something to it. Even the briefest meditation—just a short relaxation and breathing exercise once a day—will strengthen your "magical muscles" and help you to function more effectively in this and other worlds. It is not the most exciting aspect of magical work. But like physical training, magical training is something that has to be done regularly.

There are many different kinds of meditation. Just about every religious system has one, and some versions can be practiced outside of any religious context. All have something in common, however: They are designed to help shift your awareness to a deeper (or higher, if you prefer) level of existence.

The physical world is full of illusions. We look around and we see conflict, opposition, and separation. We habitually separate the magical from the mundane, and spirit from matter. Even if we know in theory that all is one, and that the world is filled with the Divine spirit, we often don't really feel it and don't really believe it.

It is impossible to *prove* the existence of the Divine, or to prove the unity of all things. However, through meditation, we can come to understand these things in a way that is outside the realm of the logical mind, though no less real.

The most basic meditation, breath counting, is a Zen technique. After you have grounded and centered, allow yourself to breathe gently and evenly. Let yourself breathe the way you would if you were asleep—without effort. Count "one" as your inhale, "two" as you exhale, and so on up to four. Then start over. Do your best to think of nothing but your breathing and your counting. Distracting thoughts will drift in; let them drift right back out. Don't get frustrated. Your measure of success is not in how long you can go without having a distracting thought, but rather in how persistent and patient you can be in your meditation. Start with five or ten minutes a day and *gradually* work up to longer periods of time, adding five minutes every two weeks. This may seem like nothing, but in our rapid-fire culture, a few minutes of quiet can seem like forever at first.

Another kind of meditation, one that is especially good for the Pagan path, is to focus completely on an object. This can be done using a lighted candle, and is great with objects from the wild, such as a leaf or stone. In this the process is the same: You're providing a focus for your attention in order to still your mind. In this case, hold the object and look at it and just allow it to exist. Make no judgments or associations. When these thoughts drift in, let them drift back out. Try it using different objects. The practice of experiencing something without judging or comparing will be very useful in your daily life.

In these meditations, you will probably have some beautiful and exciting thoughts and understanding. In a strict Zen practice, you would be taught not to take them too seriously; that they are just your brain's way of trying to distract you from the stillness that is your goal. Since I'm not a Zen monk, I will be a heretic and say that meditation is a great way to directly experience a Mystery. Stillness is one of those Mysteries, but it is the center of a spiral around which we like to dance. The journey inward is just as important as the center itself. So if you have a moment of enlightenment while meditating, enjoy it, then store it away to think about later, and go right back to your practice of breath counting or contemplation.

Meditation teaches the ability to be passive and receiving, qualities virtually ignored in Wicca. We Pagans and Witches are always setting up elaborate rituals, doing spellwork, dancing, drumming, reading—we hunt after Deity as if it were deliberately trying to hide from us. The Eastern paths teach that all we need to do is essentially shut up for a few minutes to realize that Deity is right here, right now. And all we need do is open our arms to welcome it.

Learn a form of divination. Divination—the use of tarot, palm reading, tea leaves, crystal balls, or runes—is often referred to as "fortune-telling," and, as an art, divination isn't usually taken very seriously. When it is, people will make the mistake of thinking that the future is written in stone—that Fate has determined the fall of the cards, and nothing can be altered.

But the future is *not* predetermined. Magically speaking, all space is here and all time is now. The time line we imagine is only one, narrow way of looking at things. Actually, possible universes stretch out in all directions—and cross infinite times. Rather than a straight line, we can think of time as a bowl of spaghetti. The decisions we make every second change our path from one strand to another.

Divination is much more than just "fortune-telling."

So what is the point of divination, if the future is always changing? Well, some futures are more likely than others. For instance,
it is possible that I could become a pig farmer in Idaho next year,
but rather unlikely. It seems to be a certainty that the sun will
rise tomorrow. Will I be a rich and famous author? Ah, that has
yet to be determined. But divination can tell me whether I'm heading in that direction. If it shows that the prospects are bleak, I
have choices to make: work harder on my writing, go back to
school and get qualified for a different job, become a vagabond,
and so on.

Of course, just the fact of knowing about a probable outcome
will wind up changing it to some extent. That's where divination is
complicated. It's useful in spotting trends, but less so in forecast-
ing certainties. When you use divination, the events shown to you
by the tool you're using are not isolated incidents happening at
some future time; they are current influences all around and
within yourself. It's a sphere, rather than a highway.

How does divination actually work? The tool you use provides a focus for your own psychic abilities to do their thing. For most people, it's very hard to just close their eyes and shift into a different state of awareness. as with the meditations above, we need a little something to move our consciousness away from the "everyday." The images can be very elaborate—many tarot decks are beautifully illustrated—or they can be a simple mirror or crystal.

> KERRI: "I've tried many forms of divination, and the only one I've had an immediate response to and connection with was tarot cards. I started as a teenager. I can find out anything through the cards. When I want to know what move I should make next, or what's going to happen tomorrow or next week, I sit by myself with a candle and I concentrate, and I think of nothing except my question. I let everything else go. As I'm shuffling, I'm pouring myself into the cards with the question. Then I pull out ten cards, and they speak right to me. At very stressful times, I'm unable to do readings, so I ask other people I know and trust to do readings for me."

Because divination relies on your own innate abilities, it *will not work* unless you are in the right state of mind. You must be relaxed and grounded. If you are particularly involved with the issue you're looking into, you will influence the reading: "Oh, the Death card—this job will mean the demise of my career. Better turn it down." or "Oh, the Death card—this job will bring a dramatic and powerful change into my career. Better go for it!" That kind of reading will certainly help you clarify what you want, but you won't get an objective view of the situation and all your options. If you feel that you can't be objective, it's better to go to someone uninvolved. Some professional psychics are very good, and some are con artists. If you can't get a reliable recommendation, you just have to choose one by "feel."

If you want to get started in divination, I recommend that you start with a tarot deck. The Rider-Waite deck is good because its symbolism is very clear, and the design of most other decks is based on this one. If you want a different deck, make sure it's illustrated, and make sure it's actually a tarot deck, with seventy-eight cards—there are a few divination decks, like some Native American and angel decks, that use a totally different system. Stick with the classic theme at first.

As far as "meanings" are concerned: You should first get acquainted with the cards themselves. After that, read the pamphlet that came with the deck and go ahead and buy some books on the tarot—but don't hold their definitions too dear. Just as with dream symbols, your own impression of the card meanings is more important than anyone else's, since you're the one doing the readings.

Trancework. Trance is similar to meditation, except that after we relax and change our consciousness, we go on a nonphysical journey to another world. There we are usually given some information or understanding about ourselves. It's sort of like inducing a dream in which you are in control (or more in control, anyway). Other times, however, we find ourselves traveling further and encountering challenges and problems that are just as vivid and real as those in the physical world. Trances are unpredictable and therefore should not be done very deeply until you become very comfortable in other worlds and with using your psychic senses.

To experiment with trancework, after you are relaxed, imagine a setting as vividly as possible. Then place yourself in it. It's good to start with something pleasant, like a forest or a meadow. Feel the grass under your feet, smell the breeze, look around. Then go for a walk. Stay under as long as you like. You will usually have a sense of when it is time to stop, but if you don't trust that, set your clock radio alarm to go off (quietly) after a short while. Fifteen minutes is enough to start with.

> STEPHEN: "My one real experience on the other side was a shamanic soul retrieval. My cat way dying, and I had tried several times to heal him. Over dinner, I had drunk a fair amount of wine and was feeling its effects. When I closed my eyes, I suddenly found myself on the shore of a river. To get across, I had to wrestle a 'guardian.' After an unsuccessful attempt, I dove under it and swam to the bottom. It did not follow. There was seaweed growing on the bottom, and I picked some. At the far shore, I had to pull myself out of the

water as if I were stuck in mud, or climbing out of a hole in the ice.

"On the other shore I spotted my cat. His back half was a skeleton. I ran after him and caught him, but his hind quarters remained skeletal. No effort on my part could change that. I caught a large 'bird' and flew back across the river. My eyes opened, and I was filled to overflowing with energy, which I knew belonged in my cat. I put both hands on him and 'let it rip.' When the flow stopped, I broke contact. He got temporarily better, but fell back into his illness in a few days. I never could get back across to find his other half."

Safety

For the same reason people go to horror movies, a lot of Witches get very dramatic about nonphysical scary things they've experienced. But much of what we see in dreams or trance is really garbage from our unconscious mind—which just means something within is asking for attention. For instance, a threatening figure you see in trance may represent a fear that has been holding you back—in which case you'll want to work on destroying it—*or* it could be an image of your personal strength and power—and you should join with it. Just because something feels frightening does not mean you need to call an exorcist.

At one time, a couple of members of my student Pagan group decided there was some kind of evil entity living in a grove of trees out by the athletic fields. They told us what it "looked" like—reptilian with bright, glowing red eyes—and soon afterward, more people in the group reported sensing something out there. I won't speculate on whether anything was actually there to begin with. However, the power of suggestion, magnified by people's fears, certainly made it real in a sense, even if it wasn't before. After a while, I started feeling some kind of presence, myself. It may have been real, but then again, thought-projections do happen.

Even if you have reason to doubt that the scary thing you're experiencing is an actual threat, it still means it's time to pause. Just because you practice Witchcraft does not make you invincible. Quite the opposite: Doing any kind of magic opens you up to influences of which you are usually not aware. This is useful and good, but it also means you are more open to harm. If you sense an actual risk, stop whatever it was you were doing, throw up a stronger shield, and return to normal consciousness. (Remember, many monsters *are* afraid of light.)

The most common-sense route is to plan for the worst. Cast a circle before you start. Ground and center. And don't swim in the deep end until you're certain you're ready for it.

One of the things that makes Wicca unique among religions is this: Instead of fighting shadows, we run to embrace them. We are willing to face the fear that the unknown brings, just for the chance to see with our eyes wide open. We know there is more to our existence than the material world; that which is most real and vibrant is unseen, just under the surface. As you progress in your magical development, you will become comfortable enough to truly exist in two worlds. And then you will see the true value of the requisite travel: not for thrills and chills, but to gain a deeper understanding and a deeper kind of power.

MARGOT: "When my friend Gene passed, I spent most of the winter afterward feeling sorry for myself. I really started to hit rock bottom emotionally. . . . And one night I basically decided that there was just no bloody point. And at about three in the morning one night, I threw some myrrh on the censer and lit some black candles and cursed out Death. I literally and out loud said, 'Fuck you, Death. You took away the only thing that mattered at all to me. Come on, you son of a bitch, take me too!'

"I climbed into bed feeling even more sorry for myself because I was pissed off now. I don't even remember closing my eyes. One minute I was lying in my bed and the next minute I was standing on a dark shore of perpetual twilight, looking out at the water. And I felt a touch on my shoulder that was so full of presence yet so light at the same time. . . . I turned around and I saw the expected very tall, very dark, cloaked-in-shadowed-personage scythe-wielder. He said to me, 'You say I stole your precious Eugene from you. But I tell you this: I take nothing that is not mine.'

"I don't know how long I was there. I'm still remembering things that we discussed, ten years later. I was shown lots of different things, some of them relating to my life, some relating to my calling that I didn't know I had at that point. We walked by the water for a long time, and talked about life, art, poetry, love.

"Just as my roommate was starting to call 911, I came to, and it hurt to take in a breath, and the light hurt, and he heard me coughing and dropped the phone and was really scared, like 'Oh my God, what were you doing awake? You weren't breathing.' And I laughed for the first time that entire winter."

CHAPTER NINE

Initiation

DAVID: "I sat skyclad on an outcropping of rock in the middle of a forest. Beneath me, a mountain stream danced and played its way over the boulders into the valley below. All around me, the trees swayed in the breeze. The air was scented with pine and the rich earth of the forest floor. The sun caressed my body with its warmth. I held my athame and introduced myself to each of the Quarters. I asked the Goddess and the God to look upon me on the path of life, in such ever direction that they chose. I swore a sacred oath to be faithful to them and to honor my fellow practitioners of the Craft and to protect our holy Mother Earth. . . . Can anyone say that their initiation was more valid than mine?"

Initiation means "beginning." It is a beginning of another phase of your life. It is a door you can choose to go through, but you must make that choice without knowing what is on the other side. And as you learned when first you breathed the cold air of this Earth, beginnings are difficult and sometimes terrifying.

There are three different types of Wiccan initiations:

1. Through ceremony, you are recognized as a member of a tradition.
2. Through ceremony, you are recognized as a member of a coven. (Sometimes goes along with number 1.)
3. Through ceremony, you state the beginning of your personal commitment to the Wiccan path. (Also called a "dedication," or "self-initiation.")

And then there is one more:

4. In the course of your ordinary life, you are put through an ordeal, or powerful experience, that produces learning, growth, and positive, permanent changes in your psyche.

It is not hard to see which type of initiation will affect you the most strongly. But ironically enough, when people ask, "Have you been initiated?" they are usually referring to the first three—ceremonies that, more often than not, simply acknowledge or commemorate a stage of learning, rather than help to bring it about.

When you are admitted into a coven or tradition, or receive a higher degree in your learning, it is a ceremony, nothing more. It means you have done the work you were supposed to do, and it may mean you now have access to certain coven secrets.

When you self-initiate, it is also a formal statement, but this time it is a statement of your dedication. You have done a lot of research, reading, thinking, and meditating, and you have decided you want to practice Wicca. The ritual is for your benefit, a way to focus your energies and celebrate your new beginning.

The fourth type of initiation, what should be called "a true initiation," is a completely different story. It does not involve ritual, and it cannot be planned by human means. The Gods alone decide when we have fulfilled the requirements, and when we are ready to graduate to the next level.

The pattern of our lives may be chaotic and unpredictable; but woven into it are some very clear boundaries. We move from one stage of life and learning into another one, and often the move is very abrupt. True initiation involves tests and challenges that are a natural but completely unpredictable part of life. There is no course of study, no practice exams, for these tests.

An initiatory experience is often unexpected and gives you no choice but to face it and work through it. There's a certain amount of fear or uncertainty in your reaction to the challenge. If you think, "no sweat," then you are not going to be profoundly affected by the change—and you won't grow as much. In an initiation, you will be called upon to use your own unique abilities—especially ones you have had to attain over time, such as strength, wisdom, and the ability to put things in perspective.

Just in the course of living, we go through initiatory experiences. Some come in the form of ordeals. They can involve serious illness, an intimidating court battle, an emotionally charged confrontation, the death of a loved one, a move to an unfamiliar place, or perhaps even losing a job.

Initiations can also come in the form of natural life challenges; less traumatic, but just as life-changing. The first, and probably most traumatic experience: your birth. Then there's making a relationship work, having a child, the sudden appearance of a great opportunity for which you might not feel ready, the struggles you go through as you create or destroy parts of your life, and even the sometimes lengthy process of psychotherapy—getting yourself together. What about puberty, your first date, marriage, aging, and, another obvious one—your own death?

Part of being a Witch is learning how to ride the waves of these changes, to use them as learning tools and opportunities to experience more of life. These are the transitions for which we craft rite-of-passage rituals. A Witch should experience her first gray hair with as much joy and excitement as she did her first menstrual period. If you are being dragged through life kicking and screaming, then you are not living in harmony with nature.

This is not to suggest that all the changes in your life should be met with bland acceptance. Sometimes the challenge lies in being able to defend yourself, such as escaping from the ordeal of an abusive relationship. Other times, it will be a struggle to come to terms with a situation, such as testing HIV-positive. It is at times when the wave of change threatens to drag you under, that you can come out on the other side truly transformed.

Are the Gods at work here? I like to think so. Somehow it's easier to imagine the Lord and Lady offering personal challenges than it is to think of these things as the "way of the Universe." If someone personal is in charge of your initiations, then you have someone to complain to when the going gets rough.

OBSIDIANA: "One night I noticed that my feline familiar, Greedy, wasn't breathing quite right. I took him to the vet, and they determined that he had lung cancer. We decided it would be best to send him off on his way.

"I stayed with him when he died, and that was hard. He had been by my side through so much. He was really sick when I saw him. I tried to explain to him why I was doing this, and I told him I would be waiting for him.

"The following day, after he died, I burnt a candle for him. I just drifted off, and Freya showed up, which I thought was kind of strange, because I was familiar with the Norse Gods and Goddesses, but I was never really drawn to them. Then I heard something that I knew was Greedy crying. And I wanted to hold him in the worst way. And I asked to hold him. I was told that it was not time for us to comfort each other, and I realized we had done that an awful lot when he was alive. I was told that I had to comfort myself, that he only cried for my anguish. I knew I was in bad shape and I knew I had a lot of work to do, but now I was being told I was doing it for him, so that he could be at peace. So there was my incentive, to try to get myself together.

"I spent the summer working on that, and a lot of times when I was working, there was that Freya energy. I remember one night being really upset because there was this huge hole in my heart and my soul that Greedy and everybody else that had died took with them. And it was like there was nothing left of me. I was gone. I remember sitting there in front of my altar and thinking about this, and wondering,

Where am I, in the middle of all this? and again, the energy of Greedy was present. And it occurred to me that the little bit that everybody took with them is like the key. That's how you recognize each other the next time around. That was very reassuring. It's like, 'I'm *not* gone. I'm out there, all over the place, and it's all coming back eventually. It's all gonna come back.'

"It was a lot of things like that, little revelations, that made it easier. The whole thing came together on Samhain when I was doing my ritual to honor Greedy. I was doing some grief work, and there was Freya again! She told me that I had done good work, and Greedy was at peace, and she said that she remembered I had wanted to hold him, and she said that I could. And this wasn't Greedy-energy, this was *Greedy*. I mean, yeah, I was in a trance, but I could smell him, I could feel him, he was there, solid. And he was purring. It was a reward, that I was allowed to do that again. And the most amazing thing was that I could hand him back, and it wasn't a struggle."

Is it possible to create a ceremonial initiation that will produce a profound and lasting effect on the initiate? The answer is yes, but it's not easy, and it won't be as powerful as the initiations that come naturally. The Gods know exactly what we're ready for, and what challenges we need to overcome in order to acquire the most learning. In order for a ceremonial initiation to have transformative effect, the person writing the ritual must know the initiate very well. He must be able to put together an experience that will include a challenge that is just difficult enough to be intimidating, but with a reasonable chance that the initiate will succeed. And the symbols involved must be relevant to the initiate's life.

As Witches, we can sometimes get carried away with the idea of our own power. Many people treat the ceremonial initiations as if they were going to be transformative experiences, when there is really no basis for that.

I learned this lesson myself at age nineteen, when I had fulfilled my requirements to be initiated first degree in my coven and my tradition. The week before my initiation, I was very nervous, didn't know the details of the ceremony. I had a basic idea of what was to happen, but was told there would be "surprises." I knew that an initiation was supposed to involve an ordeal and a challenge. Would I make it through?

That night I was both excited and terrified. I had a ritual bath to cleanse myself and to emotionally and mentally prepare for the ceremony. There was soft music and candlelight. Scented oils and aromatic herbs floated in the steaming water. This was my special night; my rebirth.

But when the time came for the ceremony, I found that the words were being read from a script. The motions were being done with one eye on the photocopied paper. There were mysterious moments, and I was certainly moved, but it was not a transformative experience. I was disappointed and disillusioned.

I had expected something to happen that night. I had expected to come out of there a changed person. But the only concrete result of my ceremonial initiation was that I could say that I held first degree in my tradition.

But that ceremony got me thinking. Within the Wiccan philosophy, initiation is very important—initiation into the tradition, to the mysteries, to the next phase of learning, the next phase of life. That was when I first realized I wanted something more than the scripted ceremony. I wanted a true initiatory experience! I wanted to be transformed! And so I began to search even harder. (Perhaps in that way, my initiation was a successful one.)

But in just the same way that the Mysteries cannot be explained, no one can tell you what it means to go through a real initiation. You may experience terrible personal conflicts, heartwrenching loss, emotional difficulties. There may be times when you find yourself in despair and confusion. And all of these times will be opportunities to grow and learn.

I won't say that I laughed all the way through these moments, when I experienced them, saying, "Oh, it's just another initiation." But, experiencing these things as a Witch, I didn't fight them. I experienced my sorrow and my anger wholeheartedly. I did my best to hold nothing back. I learned whole new depths of emotion. And sometimes I didn't think I'd get to the other side, but I did. And then I was able to see how much I had grown.

You should always expect new initiations and new challenges, and they will be just as difficult, if not more so, than the ones you first undergo. And you may be afraid of them. But your decision to go through that door is part of what makes you a Witch.

LAUREL: "As eclectics, in the groups that I was with then . . . an initiation was anything from unnecessary hierarchical drama to a sublime personal sacred experience. I myself find that an initiation is an opening of doors, not politically but emotionally and spiritually. As a Gardnerian, I find them to be great safety valves. They mark a level of learning and experience that you can share with others, that you know others have passed through. And that those who you help will pass through them in their turn.

"I've had rites of passage that I've both participated in and been the victim/guest-of-honor of. When the experience has been lacking, it's mainly been either an instance of personal expectations not being met, or the imposition of others' expectations being forced upon you. When the experiences are positive, whether the ritual was designed to be done to you, for you, or by you, what makes it work is you. You have to be open and willing to accept whatever comes.

"It's always been somebody's opinion, some bit of politics, some bit of feminism or nonfeminism that has slipped into the ritual that jangles your nerves because it's not part of you, it's part of another. The solution is the people you choose to have around you at the time of any rite of passage. There has to be mutual respect, there has to be perfect trust. Without those two things, you're not going to be able to do anything after your initiation, let alone before."

Self-Initiation

I started practicing Wicca at age sixteen. I was not initiated into a coven until I was nineteen years old. Does that mean that during those three intervening years I was not a real Witch?

That I was not qualified to practice the Craft? That I was just rehearsing?

In the early days of the Craft, formal, ceremonial initiation was extremely important to many people. It was a way of confirming that you had a commitment to the path, and that someone else would vouch for your sincerity. It also had the advantage of ensuring that a more-or-less "pure" tradition was being taught and carried on.

But in the half century since then, the Craft has grown enormously. There are still hundreds of covens that put their students through standard initiations and pass on rituals and knowledge started way back when, in the beginning of their tradition. However, covens like this seem to be in the minority these days. Now that there are more and more books on Wicca on the shelves, people are no longer dependent on "secret" manuscripts that can only be obtained upon initiation into a coven. The information is easily available—even including some rituals and initiations that were originally meant to be kept within the tradition. (Of course, it is sad that in order for these materials to be passed on, an oath had to have been broken somewhere.)

Now absolutely anyone can practice the Craft. You don't have to know anybody, you don't have to enter into a course of study, and you don't have to make any commitment. This is a double-edged sword. It's good for people who are under eighteen, or who live in isolated areas, or who want to start their own tradition, or who can't find a coven they like, or who just prefer to practice solitary. On the other hand, it also demands a lot of responsibility on the part of the individual: He must do a lot of reading, meditating, practicing, and celebrating on his own, without a teacher to help him out. (Well, except the Gods, but you have to know how to listen to them.)

The one great thing about the do-it-yourself approach is that you can practice any damn way you like. You are not restricted to a tradition; you can take bits and pieces from all the books you read and maybe the different people you talk with, and put together your own system.

There may still be a few people who scoff at the self-taught

Witch, but their numbers are dwindling. There are now covens that began when one person picked up a book on Wicca and said, "This is neat!" and those covens have birthed several new generations.

If you have made the choice to go it alone, or even if you simply haven't found a coven yet, you may want to do a self-initiation, or a "dedication." This is simply a ritual you write and perform that will formalize your entrance into the Craft. It is a way to introduce myself to the gods, and to make a point of switching your way of thinking into a magical one. You may want to be able to say, "Yes, I am a Witch."

Can you be a Witch without having gone through any kind of formal initiation or dedication? Of course. But if you want to do a self-initiation, read on.

> LORRIE: "I was initiated by my High Priestess, but from that point on she made me feel that somehow she was responsible for all the Craft things I became good at. Like if it wasn't for her I wouldn't have succeeded to be a true Pagan or something. When I moved to the mountains I did a self-initiation at the local waterfalls that really felt 'right.' "

Self-Initiation

This ceremony is performed to mark the beginning of your life in the Craft. It should only be done when you have decided to make some measure of commitment to this path. If you are still reading and considering, it isn't yet time to take this step.

If you feel sure that you want to perform a self-initiation, think about your motivations. Why do you want this? Do you think it will make you more powerful? Bring you closer to the Gods? Make you legitimate? Make someone like you? Help you to see things more clearly? Are you just looking for a powerful, magical experience? Consider for a while whether you think your reasons are good ones, and why.

Here follows a simple outline for a self-initiation. Most of the rite-of-passage ceremonies we go through in our lives are prewritten; graduations, christenings, weddings. How many time have you heard the words, "To have and to hold, from this day forward"? Beautiful and poetic, for certain—but not written with any particular individual in mind. They have become generic.

You should make your own initiation personal and as powerful as possible. Improvise on this outline; don't just use it as is. Make sure that you will be alone and undisturbed for at least two hours. The ritual itself won't take that long, but you will need time to prepare, as well as time to sit and relax afterward.

First, thoroughly clean the space you're going to be using. It is important that you enter your new life in a pleasant environment. As you tidy, scrub, vacuum, and dust, imagine yourself cleansing the space of all negative energy and releasing the past.

Next, make the physical changes in your environment that will help you make the transformation into sacred space. You might want to light candles, put on music that you find meditational and inspirational, or burn incense. Remember: This is not a sabbat ritual, and it not a ritual for a magical working. It is your own rite of passage, and that is the focus you should keep when you're getting the room ready.

Gather together all the materials you will need for the ritual. This is going to include:

1. Anything you would normally put on a ritual altar.
2. Images of birth (eggs and the color red, for instance).
3. A symbol or photo to represent yourself.
4. Something to represent your old life (something from your childhood is ideal).
5. Something to represent your new life (something new, something that you associate strongly with your practice of the Craft).
6. Something to eat and drink (wine and cakes are traditional, but you can improvise).
7. Scented oil.
8. A bowl of saltwater.

Next, it's time to prepare yourself. Nudity is appropriate at an initiation. You are going through a death and rebirth. You should appear to the Gods exactly as they made you, hiding nothing. Even groups that practice clothed often initiate people skyclad. People are instructed to remove everything, even jewelry. A remarkable emotional change happens when you are completely naked. You are vulnerable, but you are also completely free and unfettered. If, however, you feel that your nudity would be so distracting and upsetting that you won't reap the full benefits of the ceremony, you can skip it. Just wear whatever you'd usually wear for ritual.

Now, turn off the ringer on the telephone and lock your door. Take a few moments to calm yourself. Relax, ground, and center. Empty your mind and focus on your breathing. Let go of your self for a few minutes.

When you feel ready, cast your circle and call the elements. Take as much time as you need. You can do this all silently if you like. Call on the God and Goddess.

Kneel, facing your altar. State your intention, either aloud or silently. You may want to meditate on this beforehand, and write down what you want to say. Why are you here? What events have led you to this place? What helped you make your decision? What are your fears or misgivings? What unique and wonderful qualities or talents do you have to offer as a gift to the Gods? *What do you want?* Speak from your heart.

Open yourself up to the loving energies of the God and Goddess and allow yourself to experience whatever response they might give. You may sense them speaking to you; you may see a vision, or your may just feel emotion wash over you. When they have given their acceptance—or when you feel it is time—stand up.

Take the bowl of saltwater from the altar. Meditate for a few moments on its significance. Salt and water represent life; they are the ocean, they are your mother's womb. But they are also tears, and death; the Dead Sea can contain no life because it contains so much salt. Sprinkle yourself with saltwater. Taste it on your tongue. Know life, and death. Imagine the salt cleansing away all that you don't need anymore—your fears, your bad habits, your old life. You are dying, and you are brand-new. You are purified. You are reborn. If you like, say some words to reinforce this in your mind.

Take the scented oil from the altar. Anoint yourself in whatever way you feel appropriate. You might wish to just place a drop upon your third eye (between your eyebrows), or to mark the points of a pentacle on your body, or to anoint the parts of yourself that seem most sacred to the Gods; for instance, your belly if you're female. Whatever you do, just do it in such a way that you feel as though you, like a magical tool, have been consecrated. If you like, say something meaningful, to acknowledge in words what you have just done in actions and symbols.

Face the east. You are not invoking here; you have already done that. The spirits of the elements are with you in the circle. You are *presenting* yourself to them as a newly initiated Witch. As a Witch, one of your goals in your worship is to be one with the forces of nature. At your initiation, you are taking the first step in the growth of that awareness.

Present yourself to fire, water, and earth. Imagine yourself joining with them. Say some sort of greeting to each direction. Proclaim yourself a Witch. You might try, "Spirits of the (direction), I (name) do present myself to you as a newly consecrated Witch. Blessed be!" Be proud, be joyful!

Now, do a blessing of the cakes and ale. As you eat and drink, meditate on the Mystery: the grain and fruit that have been cut down, that have died, now nourish you and give you life. By eating and drinking, you become part of the cycle; you take in life and you take in death. There is no separation between you and the Gods, just an endless balanced cycle.

When you are done, sit quietly in whatever position you feel most centered. Give yourself time to absorb the ritual you have just performed. Meditate on the symbols of your old life and on your new life. No one can predict what you will be feeling at this time; you may be tremendously moved, or you may be bored and think, Is this it? Whatever you think or feel, give it time. You may not notice anything different in yourself for days, and then all of a sudden it will hit you. It may be more gradual. It may be more subdued, just a quiet feeling of pride and belonging.

When you feel you have finished, thank the God and Goddess, dismiss the elements, and close the circle.

But remember not to place too much importance on this kind of initiation. It is most of all a beginning, a statement of intent. The rest is up to you. You make the commitment to live as a Witch, you decide what that means to you, you renew your commitment every second of every day. Your self-initiation is about your own identity as a member of the Craft.

As far as those initiations the Gods bestow—what can be said, but HEADS UP!

CHAPTER TEN

Everyday Magic

UGRIC: "Years ago, I felt that you obtained information and then you sat on it. There's an old saying, 'Read one book, you know something. Read two books, you're an expert. Read three books, you're a master.' Years ago, I believed that— before I had my first shamanic experience. After that, I was showed that the world is indeed a very different place from what I saw in books."

It's easy to be a holy man on a mountain, and it's easy to be a Witch in circle. Surrounded by candlelight and with no distractions, it's no trouble to slip into a magical state of mind. But if we can only use our magic at certain times in certain conditions, it's practically useless. Your religion is not just a name or a label, it says something about the way you live. When you are a Witch, it means you are living a magical life every day—both in and out of circle.

The term *everyday magic* has sometimes been used to mean that the ingredients for spells are easy to find. That should be a given. Here it specifically means doing magic in what may seem a "mundane" setting; at work, driving in your car, while doing chores. When you perform everyday magic, you are bringing into your daily life the same sense of wonder and mystery and strength you feel in circle.

Sacred Living Space

We create sacred space before we cast a circle, to shift our awareness into a deeper state, and to make a space where we can feel safe. Here it means that your home, room, or apartment is dedicated to the Gods and to your own spiritual growth. It's a place in which you feel completely safe and comfortable, and a place in which you feel free to create—whether that means cooking, drawing, rearranging furniture, or casting spells.

There are many magical and physical ways to transform a living area into sacred space. Chances are you've already done some of these without knowing it. You have probably decorated your apartment or room in ways that reflect your personality and make you feel good. If this applies, think about what you've done. What things in your space do you think work really well? Which things are you proud of? What things about your space bother you? What things can you change?

When, as a teenager, I switched bedrooms with my mother, my new room was painted bright yellow. Canary yellow. My mother said the color lifted her spirits, but it just made me tense. So I asked if I could paint the room a different color. Mom agreed to pay for the paint, but that was all. After a lot of thought, I chose the color myself (a pale beige) and did most of the painting as well. Even before I became a Witch, I discovered one of the most important magical techniques: Working on something with your own hands makes it yours. I absolutely loved the room this way, and I found that I was able to do a lot of other things with it once the walls were the "right" color!

 EXERCISE: Creating a Permanent Sacred Space

> Get yourself a large piece of plain white paper. Close your eyes and imagine your "ideal" room. If you're feeling ambitious, imag-

ine a whole apartment or house of your own design. Location, money, even materials that haven't been invented yet—anything is possible. If you are a visual or artistic person, go ahead and draw what you imagine. You could also describe it in words. Fill your space with any objects or people. If you want it to be underwater or on a mountaintop, fine. Stretch the exercise out over a couple of days if you need the time. And be honest.

When you're done, you will have learned things: First, you will learn a lot about yourself, what you like to surround yourself with, what things please you, and what do not. Also, you will have an idea of what changes you can make to your space to make it a better place for you to live in. For instance, if your ideal room would be underwater, you could paint the walls of your space blue-green, or decorate in that theme. Finally, you will have a better idea of your own magical style.

When you create ritual, you are changing your surroundings to change your frame of mind. Now that you have an idea of the kind of space that you would enjoy living in, think about the ways in which you could change your space to change your mood. For instance, what different colors could you decorate in to calm yourself down or to get yourself psyched up? You can experiment with this when you meditate by changing the color of your altar cloth. You may be surprised with the results when you expect a certain color to relax you and instead it makes you tense.

The Household Altar

KERRI: "On the altar, I keep my candles, my censer, a bell, God and Goddess statues, an athame, a wand, an incense burner, a cup, and a bowl with salt. Sometimes I'll change the herbs or incense depending on what I'm going to use for a spell, or what I'm hoping for. But other than that, those tools are always on my altar. The only tool I ever take out of my permanent circle is my athame."

Many Witches like to have a permanent altar in their living space. It can go on a shelf, on top of a table, TV, stereo, or dresser. It's meant to remain set up all the time, though it can and should be changed around according to your needs.

The altar I had in my bedroom as a teenager.

You can decide for yourself how "sacred" you want your household altar to be. Some people get upset when guests rest their Coke cans on the altar; others don't draw such a distinction between the altar and the rest of the furniture.

Many people keep statues of the Gods and their magical tools on their altars. But if you are concerned about other people messing around with these things, consider keeping your magical tools elsewhere. One of the best things about a household altar is that you don't have to make it "appropriate" for an occasion or working. It can include whatever symbolic objects and personal things you like.

These things might be included: photos of friends and relatives, candles, crystals and stones, an incense burner, special or sacred jewelry, symbols of things that are important to you (a pen if you're a writer, tuning fork if you're a musician; maybe a baseball if that's your thing!), seasonal decorations such as Indian corn or spring flowers, copies of poems or song lyrics, gifts from people you care about, and so on.

You also can (and should) change it around every now and then, or perhaps create one thing to focus on, to suit your state of mind or place in life. For instance, if someone you love has just died, you might create a memorial by placing his photo on the altar and decorating it with things you associate with him. If you have just gotten a degree, center your diploma there. Fill the altar with images from your school days, and symbols of what is to come. Your altar is a reflection of you and a celebration of you. Literally and figuratively, don't let it get dusty. I think it's better not to have a household altar at all, than to have one sit there neglected.

Because of all the energy and thought you put into it, the altar will become the focus of all the magic in your living space. It will function like a hearth: as the heart of your home, full of warmth, strength, beauty, and usefulness. If you take care of it, just as you would tend a fire, it will be a constant energy source. You can use it to charge items for various magical purposes. For instance, if you want to bring an amulet with you for help in a difficult situation, you could put it through a ritual purification and charging and then leave it on your altar for a few days or so beforehand. Or you could take a photograph of a friend who has asked for healing and leave that on your altar. You may want to do more, but at least the items will soak up lots of good, strong energy just from sitting there.

Magical Thinking

But enough of all this *Good Housekeeping* stuff. You don't spend twenty-four hours a day in your home. Everyday magic is about changing the way you think.

Visualization, intent, and energy are the keys to effective spellwork. Unfortunately, many of us are best at these techniques when we're worried and anxious. We visualize the worst and brace for the worst, and in so doing we're performing powerful magic without even realizing it. And the outcome isn't pretty.

Changing your thinking is not about trying to completely *eliminate* negative thoughts; that would be unhealthy (and unlikely, without invasive brain surgery). It's about listening to the way your mind works. If you catch yourself thinking yourself into a hole, don't get upset about it, simply *shift your focus*.

Remember that emotions are a natural part of being human, even ones that may seem "bad." Learn to recognize the difference between true feelings of sadness and anger, and those feelings you have created out of habit. There are, of course, zillions of self-help books about the "right" way to think. Peruse them if you like, but it will all come down to one basic idea. Be as true to yourself as possible, and do your best to avoid ways of thinking that work against you.

⊱ EXERCISE: Magical Makeover

1. Write *Magical Makeover* at the top of a page in your journal. What areas of your life do you find difficult, challenging, annoying, or just plain impossible? Make a numbered list. Don't even think right now about magic or solutions; just have a gripe session. This can include work, school, family, relationships, even things about yourself that you don't like, or want to change. Keep writing until you can't think of anything else.
2. Pick one of the worst things on the list, something that has been a real problem for you, something you have tried to fix with no success. Write that on its own page. Now make a numbered list below that, of *all* the possible solutions to the problem. For instance:

I Hate My Job

   1. Get a new job
   2. Learn to like my job
   3. Win the lottery
   4. Marry a rich person

Now you're ready to tackle the problem, using magic and common sense. To be really ambitious, you can try all the solutions at once. But it might be better, at least at first, if you just chose one solution (or a combination of two), and put all your energy there.

Use a bit of common sense, of course. You could spend all your spare money on lottery tickets, fancy clothes, and dinners at the local country club's "singles' night." But it might be more effective if you chose number 1 or 2. Let's start with number 1, "Get a new job." The most effective kind of work includes both magical and physical elements.

3. Make a heading, *Magical*. Using your magical knowledge, and your knowledge of yourself and what you want, craft a spell. Write down the materials you'll need and what you want to do. The more specific, the better. But don't stop there. Can you

think of any meditations or affirmations that would help you be more open to new opportunities? An amulet you could make? Think of all the magical ways you could draw a new job to you. Write them all down, without censoring anything.

4. Make a heading, *Physical*. Write down anything you could do on the physical plane to get yourself a new job. This list could get really long, so try to limit it to methods that you think are likely to work. It could include reading the Sunday newspaper employment section, sending out resumés, using personal contacts you have, and possibly continuing your education.

5. Now make a heading, *The Plan*. This should include what you're going to do immediately (maybe a change in thinking), short-term plans (get a Sunday paper, buy the materials for the spell), longer-term plans (cast the spell and send out resumés), and long-range plans (go back to school to advance your career).

6. Now stop writing in your journal and start working, until you have made the changes you want! You may have instant results, you may not. Be patient. It will be worth the wait. In the future, you do not always have to be quite so systematic as this. But it helps to use this method in the beginning, until it becomes second nature.

This may seem like a lot of trouble. Then you have to ask yourself, how badly do you want things to change? Magic or no magic, apathy and resignation will get you nowhere.

Magical Maintenance

RAINBOW DARKLY: "I have been chronically ill since about the age of five. I had lupus. So I used to have fevers and be constantly sick and be totally exhausted. At one point I was considered totally disabled; I was on SSI. It wasn't until I became involved in Wicca and magic and energy work, that I started actually being able to accomplish anything—and to get through a whole day functioning. And the more energy work and magic I've done, and since I've dedicated myself to the Goddess, I have been getting steadily healthier—which is still sickly compared to a lot of my friends—but I hold a full-time job and can work overtime, and can have a life besides."

It is not always necessary to sit down, write out a spell, plan the date and time, go shopping for ingredients, create sacred space, and do the working. Sometimes it helps to make a big deal out of a spell, if it's something that is very important and requires a lot of power and concentration. But consider this: You take good care of your physical body every day, so you only have to go to the doctor or hospital once in a while. Similarly, there is a general level of magical maintenance that can and should be done all the time.

Just as you can get into the habit of thinking magically, you can do workings all day every day, until doing so becomes second nature. Think about a typical day for you; many of the things you do are rich in symbolism. For instance, a shower is a cleansing. Eating lunch grounds and nourishes your energy.

Let's say you wake up one morning feeling really anxious about a job interview you have later that day. You take a few deep breaths as you ground and center in bed, imagining the covers as a protective shield that will stay with you even after you get up. You get into the shower and see the water washing away all your fears and insecurities. You get out and make yourself a cup of coffee. As you sip the drink, you take strength (and alertness!) into your body. When you get dressed, you put on a color that makes you feel calm and confident.

There are no candles, no incense, no mystical words or incantations. This is magic at its most basic level: using symbols and visualization to direct your will.

Here are some other situations that can be used for magical purposes:

- *Eating and drinking.* Replenishing your personal energy. You can also imagine the food or drink to embody any quality you want to take into yourself, i.e., peace, happiness, confidence, or love.
- *Going for a walk.* Reconnecting with Nature and the Gods. Depending on the weather and the time of day, you can use it for different needs. For instance, going out in a storm is a good time to commune with the darker aspects of Deity. Walking is also just a good way to clear your mind and calm down.

- *Cleaning.* Obviously, cleansing. Scrubbing a bathtub is also a great way to release anger or frustration in a positive way.
- *Lighting a candle.* Calming, shifting into a magical frame of mind.
- *Playing Music.* Whatever mood or quality you want to call on, choose your song accordingly. This can be very powerful—especially when you are playing an instrument or singing along.
- *Taking out the garbage.* Take along your fears, bad habits, and emotional baggage as well. Leave them out there.
- *Using the toilet.* Grounding, or releasing negative energy. This is one of the best quickie spells I know.
- *Driving.* Moving toward a goal. A lot of people find that it's also a good way to clear the mind.

You can also come up with mini spells that aren't things you'd normally be doing, but are too brief to warrant going through a whole circle-casting. Write an affirmation and put it on the wall. Change the color of your altar cloth. Burn a candle in a significant color. If you think you need a little extra insurance, you can put up a quick circle just by visualization. Don't use more energy to prepare and cast the circle than you would be using for the spell—that is a waste of time and magical energy.

Finally, a cornerstone of everyday magic is doing some kind of daily devotion when you get up and right before you go to bed. Stand at your altar (or any other place you feel is inspirational) and just breathe for a few minutes. Ground and center, hang out with the Gods, replenish your shields. Even a few minutes a day makes a huge difference.

Wicca in the Workplace

One of the biggest stumbling-blocks to living magically is the habit of mentally disconnecting our work from our "real" life. But if you work forty hours a week, that's one-third of your daily life! And goodness knows, we can all use some magic in the workplace.

Working as a Witch means two things:

1. *Find work that you find spiritually fulfilling*. That can be anything from accounting to sanitation, as long as you can feel fulfilled.

VICTORIA: "One of the greatest gifts this year has been combining my professional life and my spiritual life. There's no conflict at all. One deepens the other, one feeds the other. I'm a student in massage therapy, and as part of my training we've also done some shiatsu [Japanese finger acupressure], training in herbology, and something called polarity, which is an energy-based healing modality. So a lot of my training in school has been in energy work and in natural healing methods. To me, it's like I'm going to 'Witch school.'"

But this is a goal, and sometimes it can take a while to reach it. In the meantime, you need to:

2. *Make your current work spiritually fulfilling*. Find something about the job you do that can be seen in a positive and constructive light. For instance, you might hate cleaning up after sloppy customers, but try seeing it as "putting things in order," and giving people the luxury of being taken care of. That can at least make the task a bit less annoying, if not actually enjoyable.

It can be difficult, particularly if you're "in the closet" at work, to remember who you are—a magical, mystical, and powerful being. My former roommate told me that whenever the stress of work started to wear her down, she would say to herself, "You're not thinking like a Witch!" Then she would almost immediately feel calm and capable. Bring a small reminder, if you can—if you can't wear a pentacle, then keep a stone or amulet in your pocket. Put an illustration of a God or Goddess on your desk. Listen to Pagan music on your tape player at lunch. Remember who you are!

When you're at work, you aren't dead or in hibernation. You are still alive, growing, and learning. If you're stuck in a job you don't like, remember that you are there for a reason—probably to learn some kind of lesson. Magical thinking means having the ability to transform the negative into something positive.

Don't Forget the Physical

CATHERINE: "I've always had an interest in preventative medicine, and herbs and growing things, and it's just gotten stronger over the years. I formalized my studies when I took a two-year therapeutic herbal studies program with David Winston. Even in the herbal studies, you don't separate physical ailments from emotional or spiritual, you have to consider the whole person and where they are, just like you have to consider yourself and where you're at. The more I've gotten involved, I've seen it's like 'right living.' Not that it's the only way, it's the way I need to live, to grow spiritually."

Pagans tend to be a pretty intellectual bunch; spending time indoors, surrounded with books; spending time outdoors, meditating under trees. For a lot of us, the occasional circle dance is the only aerobic exercise we get. It's ironic that so many practitioners of a religion that recognizes the material world as sacred, neglect the physical self. Just as we fight to protect and nurture our planet, the embodiment of the Goddess, so we should take care of our own bodies, the home of our souls. We don't protect the environment solely because we need a place to live—we do it also because we recognize its deeper holiness. And so we should respect and take care of our bodies, not to live to age one hundred, but because we are the perfect image of Deity, and Deity deserves no less.

Our Pagan ancestors didn't have to worry about physical fitness. They went on day-long hikes to find food. If they didn't move, they couldn't survive. In our technologically advanced world, many of us walk from the car to the couch to the bed, to the car, to our desks at work. Let us not neglect the element of earth in our practice: strength, practicality, the physical body.

There's no need for fancy equipment, and we needn't all became aerobics instructors or Olympic athletes. A half-hour of exercise a day, whether it be walking, stretching, yoga, or swimming, is enough. Many people I know have pointed out the absurdity of driving downtown to a gym, only to spend an hour walking on the treadmill. It's a waste of energy, and it's bad for the planet. Being Pagan means being closer to the Earth. Anyway, think of how it would put you in touch with the elements if you were outdoors, walking or jogging, for a half-hour every day.

Humans like to simplify things. Either we are successful materially or we are successful in spirit. That's easier to understand, but ultimately it doesn't work. Part of being Pagan means being able to appreciate the complexity of life. It may seem like a lot to keep track of. It may seem like an impossible job, trying to be healthy physically, emotionally, mentally, and spiritually. But, hopefully, over time it will become easier, and the different elements of your life will blend into a coherent whole.

KERRI: "I treat everything with respect. When I was younger, I wouldn't think twice about tossing something out the window, and when I saw someone hugging a tree on the news I'd kind of laugh at them. Before, I could never understand the bond that we have with all living things. I make it a point not to forget this. Everything I do, I take conscious thought in what I'm doing, what the effects will be, whether it will harm anyone or anything."

The magic you weave into your world does not happen in a series of isolated incidents. It is an organic process. The changes you make in your behavior will be subtle, but the effects will be real. Magic is not really anything miraculous. It's about changing your way of thinking, and living a purposeful and sacred life.

PART THREE

The Crone
Living as a Witch

We call on you, O Crone,
As she who challenges;
We know your ancient watchful eye is open,
We know the winding path ahead is steep.
You, who hold the Mysteries within you,
You, who draw the darkness 'round the fire.
Bring to us wisdom of your journey,
Teach us where our hidden power lies.

CHAPTER ELEVEN

Community

LAUREL: "Around here, you don't have to go through any sabbat without company. I mean you'd really have to work hard at it. You have all the shops that have open sabbats and classes and seminars, and go to any Renaissance festival, any theater group, any college campus, you're bound to bump into somebody. The only hard part is getting the courage to go out there in the first place."

Even if you don't know one other Pagan, you are still a member of the Pagan community. It may sound sentimental to say so, but a community isn't only the people on one particular street or in one particular neighborhood. It can be any group with a common bond. The membership is not about where you are, but *who* you are.

Since there are still no mostly Wiccan neighborhoods, how do people find each other and get together? Through covens, groves, study groups, student organizations, metaphysical shops, Internet groups, correspondences, festivals, books, magazines, and newsletters—to name just a few ways.

The Craft community is often viewed in two contradictory ways:

1. As a mystical, mysterious, secret society—with rules, strict hierarchies, initiations, secrets, and Important Magical Work to be done. It is adults-only, and very serious stuff.
2. As the religion of the common people—with festivals, games, songs, bonfires, and lots of children. No one is excluded, and the main focus is celebration.

Wicca, as Gerald Gardner envisioned it, was not the religion of the common people; it was a mystical tradition open only to a select few who showed their worthiness. He had adults-only covens and stressed an all-important vow of secrecy. The Book of Shadows was available only to initiates. In Gardner's Craft Laws there seems to be a constant fear of being "discovered" or "captured."

It is, of course, much harder to destroy a group that is decentralized and that keeps all its information hidden. It is hard to tell whether this preoccupation with secrecy came from a true threat to the Witches in Gardner's time, or whether it simply stemmed from a romanticized view of past persecutions such as the Salem Witch Trials or the Spanish Inquisition—or both.

Secrecy is necessary in cases where you can be pretty certain your religion will be held against you: in some very conservative areas of the country, or if you are involved in a child custody dispute. And, in all cases, people have the right to keep their religious practices private.

Children should probably be left out of any possibly frightening rituals, as well as those requiring a reasonable amount of concentration or deep trance states. Likewise, if the group is doing a particularly difficult spell, raising a lot of energy, or doing an elaborate pathworking, it's probably not the best time to invite your curious non-Pagan cousin to circle.

Historically speaking, however, the Old Religion of Europe was a family affair. It was an integral part of daily life, not something done only on certain days or in certain groups. There have always been mystics, people who go further in their spiritual quest and who attempt more elaborate rituals and workings. But they are the exception. Wicca as a tradition should be for everybody, and then people can decide how involved they want to be and to what level they are going to take their own training.

In the early days of the Craft, the only way to meet other Wiccans was by joining a coven—if you could manage to find one. Now, the huge numbers of books available, the open circles and festivals, and even Pagan radio shows are bringing the religion of the common people back to the common people. Coven membership is no longer a prerequisite for community membership.

When hundreds of people gather for the maypole dance at Rites of Spring, or the bonfire at Starwood (Pagan festivals), they often come from many different traditions. Some may have been in the Craft for twenty years; some may have just come along to the festival with a Pagan friend. They are brought together by the simple act of celebration and rejoicing in the springtime. There are no requirements, no secret languages, no "insiders" or "outsiders."

Whenever anyone is doing ritual or magic, celebrating the Earth, or just generally living as a Witch, she is a member of the Pagan community—even if she has never met another person who practices as she does. When she steps between the worlds, she is joining there with all the others who are in circle at that moment. As Witches, we cannot and will not be bound by appearances!

If this is so, then why do Witches gather together at all? Isn't it enough to be united by our magic? Well, there are many reasons for becoming involved in the Pagan community:

First, Pagans are members of a minority religion. Christians and Jews in this country have the joy of celebrating their holidays with others who share their beliefs. "Merry Christmas" is something on almost everyone's lips during the month of December. Sometimes we just want to be able to say "Blessed Samhain" to someone and see the recognition in his eyes.

The Pagan community gives Witches a chance to feel "mainstream." It's not necessary to wear a pentacle at a festival; that you are Pagan is a given, or you wouldn't be there. Also, your beliefs and commitment tend to be strengthened when you see them reflected in others. When you come home from a Pagan gathering, you know that Pagans are real, that there are others who share your feelings, that you belong, and that you are all working magic.

And some things are just better done in a group. Alone, you can be joyful, but it is awfully difficult to rise to the same level of silliness and rowdiness that a good maypole dance can foster. (If you can do that all on your own, then I'd really like to meet you!) You don't have to go out and join a coven in order to have this experience. Open circles, study groups, and festivals provide plenty of opportunities to get a feeling of community.

In 1992 I attended an outdoor ritual in Salem, Massachusetts, that was a tercentenary memorial for the Witch Trials. At the end of a procession to the open field where most of the hangings had taken place, at least one thousand Witches and Pagans stood in a huge circle under the stars, holding candles. This group was composed of some traditional covens, but there were also a fair number of open circles, college groups, and solitaries in attendance. It was very powerful.

You will discover another reason to get involved in the community when you attend festivals or open circles regularly: Pagans are an unusually creative and intelligent bunch. This fact is manifested in the dozens of magazines and newsletters—remarkable, considering our relatively small numbers—the crafts and artwork; the constant creation of new rituals, chants, and meditations; and in the most flourishing element of all, the modern "bardic tradition." There are some very well-known Pagan musicians at work today, including the excellent choral group MotherTongue and artists such as Serpentine and Charlie Murphy.

But the more noteworthy part is this: It's not just professionals doing this stuff. At any bardic circle, you'll see regular folks in the community performing original songs, often without benefit of musical accompaniment. Those who play instruments bring them along to circles and festivals. There are many dedicated drummers, who use their rhythms not only for fun, but to get closer to the Gods. There is also some great Pagan satire, from "All My Avatars" (the soap opera in *Enchante* magazine), to the Wombat

Many Pagans are also craftspeople. Here are some of the incredible leather masks made by Jeff Grosky.

Wicca tradition, to the more than five hundred verses that are sung to "Old Time Religion." Our creativity and our ability to laugh at ourselves are two things that I believe will ensure our survival as a tradition.

We can also learn from our community. It's great to read books and be inspired by the Gods on your own—but joining with others can engender an extremely dynamic and exciting kind of learning. Attend the circle of a different tradition. Go to a workshop on a topic you know nothing about. Get into a heated discussion with someone who worships differently. No two people practice their religion in exactly the same way. And because the Craft is a tradition that is being formed and reformed as it grows, there's a lot of room for debate. Considering contrasting viewpoints is essential in developing your own spirituality. You will either revise your beliefs, or they will become reinforced and stronger as they are.

The community also offers the potential to make personal connections. If you are looking for a life partner, you may want this person to share your beliefs. The number of eligible Pagan singles in a bar on any given night will probably be rather low—and those who are there may not want to publicize their affiliation. Attending an open circle or festival increases your chances of finding a Pagan life-mate. These are also good places to look for friends, hiking partners, playmates for your children, or a Pagan lawyer to take on your religious harassment case.

However, the single most important reason to be involved in the community is to influence the future of the Craft. We can help to direct the growth and change of our religion. Magically speaking, our actions count, even insignificant ones. You don't have to form a Wiccan Advocacy League, but you can join an existing one, or just volunteer a few hours of your time.

Wicca is no longer a fringe movement; it is growing at an amazing rate. When most Wiccans were young and single and their tradition was intended just for them, it didn't matter how much communication occurred between groups. There was little need for pamphlets, documentaries, or conferences. But now we are in the midst of a Pagan baby boom. For the next generation's sake, we must develop some cohesion and work toward the future. That way, children will someday be able to wear a pentacle to school without being sneered at.

This change in attitude has already started. The most striking example of this was the strong Pagan presence at the Parliament of the World's Religions, an interfaith gathering that took place in Chicago, in August 1993. The parliament met first 100 years before, and at that time the new religion presented to the American public was Buddhism. This time, it was Neo-Paganism. If Wicca were still just a scattering of isolated groups, and if it were not for the existence of organizations such as the Covenant of the Goddess and the Earthspirit Community, there would have been no Pagan representation at the parliament. This was a landmark event, and our participation in it was a crucial step toward the acceptance of Wicca, and Neo-Paganism in general, as a legitimate religious tradition.

So where to start? How can one individual make a contribution to the community? Advocacy is not only about marches, rallies, and pamphlets. One way to be an advocate is simply to live as a Witch, without hiding your religious identity. Also consider organizing or participating in group meetings and gatherings; spiritual teaching; midwifery; doing advocacy work on TV, or in newspapers and magazines; setting up a Pagan bulletin-board-system or Website; working in a Pagan bookstore; sharing your creativity in the form of art, music, dance, drama, or ritual; and helping out at festivals and other gatherings by doing cooking, cleaning, childcare, or administrative work—basically, any contribution that you could make in your own hometown can be extended to the Pagan community.

Who Are the Pagans in Your Neighborhood?

TOM: "When I'm out and I see people wearing silver jewelry, I always look at it to see if it's Pagan-oriented. It's kind of a habit. If you do meet someone who has it, you do kind of the 'jewelry dance.' Like, 'Hi, nice pentagram,' 'Oh, I like your triskele,' . . . and there's embarrassed silence, and then you strike up a conversation."

You may think you're the only Pagan in your neighborhood, but you're probably wrong. They're right under your nose, and you just have to know how to look for them. Here are the standard ways of getting into the community, in order of the increasing level of your commitment and interest, capped with the option of joining a coven. Not everyone wants to be a member of such a formal group, and that doesn't have to be your ultimate goal, but if you do, these steps are a good way to get there.

1. FIND A METAPHYSICAL BOOKSTORE. Look in your yellow pages under "Bookstores," "Metaphysical," "New Age," "Occult Supplies," or even "Witchcraft." In liberal areas of the country, you shouldn't be more than an hour's drive from a New Age or occult bookstore. New York City, for instance, has several. Keep in mind that there are New Age bookstores and there are Wiccan/Pagan bookstores—and the two can be radically different. For instance, many New Age bookstores will carry books on "Goddess Worship" but none on Wicca per se. Obviously you stand a better chance of finding Pagans at a Craft bookstore than at a New Age one.

When you get there, look for the bulletin board. There will be flyers and advertisements for all sorts of gatherings, as well as notices from people looking for contacts and roommates. If you're feeling brave and/or lucky, put up a flyer of your own. Common sense dictates that you use a post office box for your correspondence. The Craft has its share of weirdos, just like any other group.

2. GET A COPY OF A PAGAN MAGAZINE.   Some are geared toward a local community, and some are more national. Inside will be advertisements for other Pagan magazines that might not be available to you except through mail order. Send away for a couple.

Besides being great sources for contacts, Pagan magazines are also valuable resources for learning. Most of the people who contribute to these publications aren't professional writers; they're just people who practice the Craft and want to share something they've learned. These magazines can help you get involved in the happenings of the community, provide ideas for your own magical lifestyle, and also give you a good laugh. If you feel inspired, you can submit an article yourself.

3. SURF THE NET.   There are a *lot* of Wiccan and Pagan sites on the World Wide Web, and a few newsgroups (try alt.pagan). The Internet is as anonymous as you want it to be, and it's a great way to have contact with other magically oriented folks, even if they live across the continent or in another country. There are even online rituals in the chat rooms of some of the major Internet providers.

4. JOIN AN OPEN CIRCLE.   Groups like New Moon New York and the Earthspirit Community in Massachusetts are active year round and have large open rituals for many of the major sabbats. These meetings are advertised in metaphysical shops and in Pagan magazines. You can also find out about them over the Internet and, of course, by word of mouth. Many people who don't belong to covens like to attend these meetings. They may not want to practice with others all the time, or may not want to make a commitment, but they like the energy of a large group ritual. Organizations like these also sponsor workshops, concerts, and so on.

5. JOIN A STUDY GROUP.   These are often advertised in occult bookstores and magazines. Many metaphysical shops have "Wicca 101" courses that cover the basics of ritual, magic, and Pagan phi-

losophy. Some shops charge a fee, and some require you to buy books at their store in order to attend the classes. Don't sign up unless you trust and respect the instructor, since it's largely his personal practice and opinions you'll be learning. If you get a bad feeling about the place or the people, don't even think twice, walk out. If you are left with no other option, it is far better to be taught only by the Gods and your own instinct than by a mediocre, unethical, or no-good person.

Some study groups are run by individuals in their homes. These rarely cost money and are usually more informal and flexible, with fluctuating memberships. Members often take turns sharing and teaching in an area of the Craft they know well. Some groups do ritual on occasion, while others meet purely for study purposes. Don't confuse a study group with a coven. No formal commitment is necessary to attend the group meetings, which generally focus on study rather than practice.

Participating in a study group is an opportunity to learn more about Wicca. And being a member of a group will be similar to, but less intense than, the experience you would have in a coven. So it will show you whether you work better in a group or solitary—even if your group doesn't do ritual.

6. JOIN A COVEN. This is not a decision to be made quickly or lightly. Becoming a member of a coven is like being adopted into a family. You may not have been able to choose your parents, but you can sure as hell decide who your High Priest and High Priestess are going to be.

Many things must be kept in mind when you're shopping around for a coven to join. First, make sure you get along with the members on a casual level. Go out for lunch or coffee with one or two of them. If you get a good feeling, *then* go ahead and guest at one of their circles. You should, of course, take into account the basic elements of their magical practice. Are they very traditional and structured? Or are they more eclectic, with a different ritual for every sabbat? However it is, make sure you can not only live with it, but also that it speaks to your soul. This is a group in which you may become an integral member, not just a guest. If you do not participate fully, you will be wasting your time.

The search for a coven to join can be a very long process. There are a number of "formal" traditions, including: Alexandrian, Celtic, Dianic, Faerie, Gardnerian, Minoan, Norse, Protean, and Seax. If you read up on each of these, you will get a general idea of what one of their covens would be like. But even within these traditions, individual covens will have idiosyncratic habits and group dynamics. Just to make things a little more confusing, most covens are "eclectic" and combine elements from one or more of the formal traditions. So you never really know what to expect until you spend some time with the people in the group, and go to a ritual or two.

When you're shopping around, here are a few warning signs:

Is money involved? Reputable covens do not ask for any money from their members, except sometimes to cover the cost of ritual materials, photocopying, and so forth. If the coven seems more like a business than a spiritual group, stay away.

Is sex involved? If you have to sleep with someone in order to receive your initiation or elevation, think twice. Some people use the Craft to sexually manipulate others. Granted, sexual initiation *can* be a valid path; but if it doesn't feel right to you, don't go there.

Has anyone you know and trust ever heard of this group? Is the group a member of a national Wiccan church, such as the Covenant of the Goddess? In order to be a member of CoG, the coven must be vouched for by two member covens, and a representative of CoG must guest at one of their rituals.

If the coven you're interested in doesn't belong to any organizations, can anyone you know give them a recommendation? There are, of course, lots of independent and beginning covens that are just fine. If no one you know has ever heard of the group, simply be more cautious.

Do they have any long-standing members? This doesn't apply to brand-new groups, obviously. But if the coven has been around for five years and has had ten different sets of members, something may be wrong. Choose a group with a low turnover rate. That will indicate stability, commitment, and wisdom on the part of the leaders and members.

Hanging out at Starwood Festival.

Do they have strong ethics? Are they politically conscious, and if so, in what way? Also, find out their viewpoint on manipulative magic. If you are going to give yourself to this group, make sure they won't take advantage of you or encourage you to do anything you feel is against your own beliefs.

Don't be in a rush to join a coven. Put your "feelers" out, then sit back and wait. Chances are, the right group will find you when it's the right time. Don't settle for anything less than a group that feels really good to you. Likewise, if you find yourself a member of a coven in which you don't feel comfortable anymore, talk things over. If that doesn't help, then leave.

At one time, the prevailing attitude in the Craft community was that if you weren't a member of a coven—if you were not being formally trained and initiated—you were not a legitimate Witch. That is no longer the case. Plenty of people choose not to join covens, for many different reasons: lack of time, the desire to keep to a personal tradition, or just the simple need for solitude. Not only are solitary Witches fully legitimate, but they can also be active members of the community.

KAREN: "I think there is very much a place for everybody. There's a tendency among some people to say, 'You're not a Witch unless you're initiated by other Witches and you're a member of a coven,' but there are solitaries, there are hierarchical covens, there are loose-knit affiliations, there are working partners, ad-hoc groups—and in many cases, it may be more healthy to move between two or more of those ways of working at any given time."

Group Ritual

KRISTINE: "When I went to my first group ritual, we got there late, and I wasn't sure whether they'd had the circle cast, or at what point in the ritual they were, or what they were doing. And we didn't know whether we had to be let in, or if we would even be accepted in, since we weren't there from the beginning. So we just kind of held back. And then when the High Priest came over, we didn't know whether he was going to tell us to leave or what. We were very relieved and happy that he asked us if we wanted to join.

"I was also relieved that people were talking. I thought it was going to be very solemn and serious. It was very comfortable. It felt good to be around other people and to know for sure that I wasn't really alone in feeling at one with the Earth, outdoors, and with Nature."

Group work, besides being fun and cozy, also packs a powerful magical punch. When people draw together and focus with one mind, the power of their magic increases exponentially. Craft legend has it that the covens of England gathered together during World War II and collectively stopped Hitler from invading. Of course, this can never be proven, or disproven. The point is that thirteen people have more psychic energy than one. And fifty people have more than thirteen. This is not to discount solitaries' magic. But there are times when you just need a greater amount of energy.

In order for group magical workings to be successful, all the participants must be on the same wavelength and have the same intent. It's even better if they know each other and are comfortable with each other. Celebratory group ritual doesn't require as much focus, but the leader still has to find a way to draw the people together.

As you can probably guess, leading a group ritual can be one of the most difficult and rewarding things a Pagan can do. If you have been practicing solitary, you may understand the concept of ritual very well; carefully chosen words and actions with symbolic meanings can have a profound effect on the individual. When you do ritual by yourself, there is only one person to affect and be affected—you. You know in advance exactly what you're going to do, and what goal you are trying to achieve. You can be reasonably certain of your outcome.

Add ten or twenty other folks, and watch the variables grow. Each person brings with him a personal life history, emotional baggage, hopes, dreams, and fears. Each sees the Gods in a different way. Each has a different amount of experience in the Craft and with magic and ritual, as well as different motives for coming to your circle. Each is looking for a meaningful magical experience.

Screwups often happen when an enthusiastic leader forgets about the other people; forgets to include them; forgets that they may have read different books or have been trained in different traditions; forgets that they get bored, tired, and hungry; forgets that they do not instinctively know how to pronounce all the God and Goddess names. He forgets that he is not alone. This will help to ensure that the next time he plans a circle, he *will* be alone.

If you are just beginning in the Craft, don't start leading group rituals until you are fairly comfortable doing them alone, or with perhaps just one other person. You'll need a basic knowledge of the structure of ritual, of the tools, and of the symbolism. You should be very comfortable with energy work, because you will be in charge of making sure the energy of the group stays contained and balanced. And you will need to be comfortable between the worlds and in the presence of the Gods—so that if you trip over the altar or accidentally drink the saltwater instead of the wine (as I have), you will be able to laugh it off.

Even if you're not planning to lead any group rituals in the near future, read this part anyway. You'll need the information here eventually. In the meantime, you can critique any circles you attend as a guest and point out (to yourself, please) all the things the High Priest or Priestess is doing wrong. Just don't take too much pleasure in it.

Well, what are you waiting for? Go ahead!

Although it may seem impossible, effective and moving group rituals happen all the time.

How to Lead a Group Ritual

You have just been volunteered by the study group leader to lead the next circle. After your panic subsides, here are some questions you'll need to ask:

1. *What is the purpose of the ritual*? Is it a sabbat, a full moon, a magical working, a rite of passage?
2. *Who will be attending*? Are they all people you know, or will there be some strangers? Is it a public ritual where anyone can show up? Will there be children?
3. *What is the experience level of the participants*? Are they mostly experienced, mostly novice, or a mix?
4. *Where will you be holding the ritual*? Indoors or outdoors; in a small space or a wide-open one?
5. *What will be the time of day*? Will you need extra lighting to read by? Will everyone be able to get back from work in time to attend?
6. *Are there any restrictions*? Is alcohol okay? Can you have a bonfire? Does it have to be quiet (for example, no drumming)?
7. *What materials do you have to work with*? Can you ask for a small donation from the other participants to help cover costs? (That three-story wicker man is going to cost you.)

Finally, the most important consideration when planning a group ritual is to make sure that everyone can be involved in some way. If you are planning a circle dance and some disabled or elderly folks will be there, ask them to drum. If inexperienced people will be attending, make sure that they won't be at a loss for what to do.

If you have been practicing ritual solitary for a while, you are used to doing everything yourself. But the others in your group ritual are not there to be your audience, they are performing it along with you. Your purpose is not to carry the weight of the circle on your shoulders alone, but to provide a structure and a focus for the others.

Some good ways of including all the participants in a group ritual are:

1. *Dancing, drumming, and chanting.* Make some noise. Dance around. Get them moving. You can organize a very specific dance or just allow people to move where they will.
2. *Making things.* This will function as a physical focus for the ritual and will also provide a token to take home. Coloring eggs at Ostara is one example.
3. *Guided meditation.* This can be as simple as talking a little about the purpose of the sabbat and then allowing people to meditate while listening to some soft music; or it can be an elaborate pathworking.
4. *Call and response.* It might seem kind of automated, but even just the repetition of "so mote it be" or "blessed be" can bring people's focus into the center.
5. *Vocal participation.* If the focus of the circle is a cleansing and renewal, have people call out those things they are leaving behind. If it is a full moon, they can call out those projects they are bringing to completion. This can be either random, or "go-around-the-circle." Random usually works better, since people don't have to feel pressured to perform when it's their turn. Instead they can join in when it seems right to them.

The symbolism of ritual must speak to the unconscious mind, or "deeper self." That's why, when planning a group ritual, you have to be as universal as possible when you choose the props and wording for your circle—but still retain the emotion and significance of the occasion.

For instance, if you call on Wodin and Freya, there may be a risk that many of the attendants will wonder, "who?" On the other hand, I have heard one invocation that called on "all the Gods and Goddesses of all the traditions of the world." It was universal, all right, but it had no power. So in the case of a God and Goddess invocation, for instance, try saying the names of the Gods you're invoking, along with some poetic and evocative words to describe their energies for those who are unfamiliar with them. Be specific, but make your intention accessible to all the participants.

Remember, just because you have associations with certain symbols, don't assume everyone else will have the same ones. You might set up a candle meditation for an Imbolc circle. Some people will see that as a peaceful image, thinking of candlelit dinners, Gothic cathedrals, and quiet evenings at home. For others, the flame of the candle will be a ravaging bonfire that consumes and destroys everything within it. To steer people in the appropriate direction, include imagery and wording that will reinforce the qualities of the symbol you want to use in your ritual. It's the difference between "the peaceful, quiet candle flame," and "the brilliant and powerful blaze of the candle."

Finally, *keep it simple*. If you are frantically trying to execute a complicated circle dance without stepping on your neighboring dancer's foot, you are not having a profound magical experience. If you want the people in circle to do something elaborate, have a rehearsal. Give everyone a copy of the words. Teach them the dance. Get all the clumsiness out of the way before you start.

The first few times you lead a group ritual, you'll probably be nervous. To minimize this feeling, first make sure you know what you're doing by getting used to solitary ritual. Then, make yourself very familiar with the ritual you have planned. Losing your place in a complex script can be very disconcerting. Better to keep it simple and have it memorized, or mostly memorized, and then keep the basic outline with you, written on an index card. At first, try to lead rituals only with people you know and trust. It's comforting to look up and see your friends all around you. And last, don't try any magical acrobatics! If you've never drawn down the moon or worked with deep trance states, now is not the time to experiment. Do the new and tricky stuff either alone or with a partner.

For me, the best part about group work is the feeling of fellowship. Some covens, and many open circles, have potluck dinners following their rituals. Others include games and activities. A couple of years ago, Duncton Wood Farm in Blairstown, New Jersey, had a game of Halloween Bingo that was almost more fun than the ritual itself (and certainly much sillier). If you start attending a coven or open circle's meetings regularly, or start going to a particular festival every year, you will get to know the people in the group. Even if you don't become intimate friends, you will still share a meaningful bond that is created through your common goal: to work magic and honor the Gods.

That brings us full circle to the topic of community. It has been said, "You shall not be a Witch alone." This means that whenever one person is living as a Witch and working magic, she is joined together with all the others on a spiritual level. But it also means that we don't *have* to be alone. The desire to form groups and to share experiences is part of human nature, and part of the spirit in which we share our magic.

CHAPTER TWELVE

Relationships

KAREN: "Most of this past year both of us have had time off, sort of a sabbatical to have to ourselves. I'm more involved in Blue Star Coven than Tom is, but we haven't evolved into a working partnership on the level that many traditions get involved in. I think it may be the sort of thing that would be very good at some stage. I think it's problematic when people think of it as 'the model' for religious and magical working."

TOM: "Yeah, you can have rituals together, but how about living magically? I mean, even the most mundane act can take on a magical aspect. Even if it's just going outside and looking up at the moon, it's not formal, but it can be magical."

Even if your Craft practice is solitary, your life is not. Beginning the serious study and practice of a new spiritual path sends ripples out through your life that touch and affect all the people who know you. Chances are, your parents will have to accept the fact that your religion is different from theirs. When you date, marry, and raise a family, you will decide what role the Craft will play in these things. Will you only choose a Wiccan partner? Will your children be brought up in the Craft? Finally, simply deciding to live as a magical person will change the way you are perceived by those around you.

Sometimes the Craft can present a threat. For instance, many people have had a hard time getting their parents to accept and approve of their practice. On the other hand, the Craft can also enhance and expand your relationships, such as when you work sex magic with someone you love. Most important, though, the Craft, kept as an integral part of your life, will help you in your relationships by helping you to view conflicts not as a pain but as a challenge—and will provide the magical inspiration to join with others in the same perfect balance as the God and Goddess.

"You're a WHAT?"

RAINBOW DARKLY: "I was raised sort of an ethnic Jew, mostly agnostic. Still, my mother did a lot to give me all the background that helped me become Wiccan. When I was little, she didn't work, and we used to take walks in the woods almost every day. I learned all the plants and flowers, said all from a strictly scientific point of view, but I learned a great love for the woods and the outdoors. She wouldn't let me pick a flower unless there were at least ten that you could see, to make sure there would be enough to seed and replenish.

"She's a research librarian, or was before she retired. And I watched her, during my adolescence, give herself the equivalent of, I'd say, at least a Master's in comparative religion. She was agnostic and she was searching. She came up with a totally different answer from mine. She has since become a complete atheist. However, I have all her neat books lying around! I had all the Greek myths from *Bullfinch's Mythology* as bedtime stories, and I got *When God Was a Woman* from her books, and then she wonders why on Earth I've turned out this way! She thinks it's rather silly and hopes I get over it soon. It's been more than ten years, and she realizes I'm not getting over it soon, and she can't understand how she raised somebody so irrational."

Those of us who weren't raised Pagan can assume that our families know just as much as the rest of the country does about Wicca—which is to say, very little. It would be great if they could approach the subject with an open mind, so that they might ask intelligent questions to try to understand what the Craft is all about. But it's a fact that the negative meanings and propaganda against magical, Nature religions and the word *witch* has existed for so long that it's no longer considered prejudice. To most people, it's simply the truth, and this puts the practicing Witch in a very difficult position. She must not only educate her family about this new religion of hers, but she is going up against years of old dictionary definitions, Halloween cartoons, fairy tales, and Satanic-cult conspiracy theories.

On the bright side, there is plenty of positive, accurate information in print about the Craft that you can use to counter the bad press. Many of the organizations listed in the appendix are happy to send you pamphlets you can photocopy and give away. If your folks are interested, they can always attend an open circle. But if they are so open-minded that they want to attend a Wiccan ritual, you've got very little to worry about!

It is possible—especially if your family members are religious Christians—that even after reading your pamphlets and listening to your explanations, they will still insist that you're a Satanist. They may believe that following any religious system other than their own will get you sent straight to Hell. In this case, it wouldn't make much difference whether you're Wiccan, Jewish, or Buddhist! If your parents are actively practicing a religion other than Wicca, they might be very disappointed and even hurt when they find that you have left the family faith. Such conflicts can't be solved overnight, but ultimately you have to follow the path you're called to follow.

Even nonreligious parents may have been frightened by all the accounts of Satanism and "ritual abuse" in the media. These stories, whether for real or not, play on a basic fear—that some huge organization is conspiring to undermine society and brainwash people. Any unknown system of religious belief can be seen as a threat. And the instinct to protect one's children can make the fear even stronger. It's understandable that your parents might react this way, but it can make your life very difficult.

If you are still in the early stage of reading, considering, and exploring, you really don't need to say anything at all—and should probably wait until you feel certain about your path. However, when you feel very strongly that you want to practice the Craft, you have a decision to make: to tell or not to tell? It depends on a lot of factors: How good is your relationship with your family? Are they hypercritical or very self-absorbed? In that case, you may have a hard time getting your point across and you may receive hostility or indifference in return. On the other hand, if you communicate well, and find them to be open-minded, you may have no problems.

Also, in what way will their religious beliefs influence their reaction? If your folks belong to a liberal church, their beliefs may actually be helpful when you have your discussion. However, if your parents are fundamentalist or orthodox in their religion, you may want to think twice about telling them at all. Chances are, they aren't going to change their beliefs, and the only outcome will be conflict.

You may also find that their lack of religion may be just as much of a stumbling block. Many people believe that all religious or spiritual paths are equally pointless and absurd. Are your parents like this? People who are not spiritual themselves can have a lot of trouble understanding why anyone would want to be. The best approach here is to just ask them to accept your faith as part of you, to respect it as your decision, and let it go at that.

Finally, how important is it to you to share this aspect of your life with your family? If you don't really feel that you and your parents have ever really understood each other or shared experiences, this may turn out to be more of the same. On the other hand, if you want to begin to understand each other, you may think discussing your beliefs is worth the risk of causing conflict.

And if you have a very open, trusting relationship with them, you harm the relationship by concealing your magical practice.

> MEILIKKI: "My mom did her best to take me around to different churches. She didn't like established religion but she didn't want to put that on me, she wanted me to make my own decision. She baptized me in the bathroom sink when I was a baby. My mom is probably the first Pagan I ever knew, but she didn't consider herself that."

The excitement you feel about your spiritual path may tempt you to go overboard in talking about it with your family. But they can easily be overwhelmed, so go slowly. When you talk with them, the goal should not be to achieve their immediate wholehearted acceptance, or to use the Craft as a battering ram to open their minds, but to arrive at a mutual understanding. Along the way you may feel angry, hurt, rejected—you may even be led to doubt your own beliefs and ideas because of things your family members say or do to you. Try to see the conflict as a test of your strength and determination, and try not to stoop to name-calling or pointless arguing.

The Conversation

> LAUREL: "I've always been a very straightforward person, and when I believe in something, I believe in it wholeheartedly, so I didn't avoid [talking to my parents about] it. It had to be taken care of right away. If they were going to kick me out of the house, they'd kick me out of the house. If not, they would either send me to be deprogrammed or they'd understand.
>
> "I put my pentacle on, came home, and went directly to my mother. I walked up to her and showed it to her. Typical of my mother, she didn't really react at first. I looked at her and said, 'Don't ask me to take it off, because I won't.' I have always done anything my mother asked me to do. She didn't say anything, and I walked away. Later that night, I heard her crying and talking to my dad, wondering where she went wrong. She knew better than to think I was going to be mixed

up in anything really bad, but also knew that I was really serious about this, whatever it was, and knowing that I'd always had a bent for parapsychology, she was worried.

"About a year later, I was in the living room with a friend of mine, and we were talking back and forth, cracking jokes, and my mom calls me into the kitchen. I walked in, and she had tears running down her face, and she gave me this huge hug. I was utterly in shock, didn't know what was going on. She looked me dead in the face, and said, 'I don't know what you're doing, I don't want to know, but I've never heard you honestly laugh before.' From that point on, she really didn't have a problem with it. Or if she did, she kept it to herself."

If you do decide to "come out" to your family, here are a few helpful hints about conducting the conversation. First impressions count, so don't jump into it. With a little forethought, and planning, you can influence the direction of the talk to be as positive as possible.

Get them at a good time. Wait until they are in a good mood and there are no distractions. Don't butter them up, but make sure they don't have anything handy to complain about. Don't talk to them if they're tired or not feeling well, or even if they're particularly excited about something else.

Don't pussyfoot around. In a similar situation, a friend of mine decided to tell her parents she was gay. She sat them down, announced in a very official voice that she had something to tell them, and got them extremely nervous. When she finally said, "I'm a lesbian," they breathed a sigh of relief. They said, "We were afraid you were going to tell us you were pregnant or you had AIDS or something really bad. You're just queer? So what!" So just remember, the way you choose to bring your message across can have a big effect on the way it's accepted.

Avoid the bombshell technique. You may believe that your family is going to react so badly that it won't matter how you tell them. That's not true. Understand that your parents are human beings with normal human reactions, and be sympathetic. Saying the word *Witch* in your first sentence will probably set a very unpleasant tone for the rest of the conversation. Don't blurt it all out just to get it over with.

The "whole truth" isn't always best. You could talk about the sacredness of Nature and the idea of the Divine embodied in each of us—without mentioning that you do your rituals skyclad. You could leave out the words *Witch* and *Pagan* altogether. If you call yourself Wiccan, Gaian, or even a "celebratory immanentist," it doesn't change the nature of what you are and what you do. Eventually you can work in the extra details, or you could just decide that your parents don't need to know everything about you, and leave it at that.

Start with something your parents can relate to. If they're interested in mythology, spirituality, alternative medicine or healing, or environmentalism; if they're feminists, if they have Wiccan friends, if they happen to like some kind of music with Pagan themes (a lot of folk music and some rock would qualify), or even if they wear crystals, you're lucky—you have some common ground. If you don't see any obvious connections, be creative and try to find something. Start talking about their interest and then bring the subject around to a corresponding element in Wicca. It's not as hard as it sounds, and it will make the Craft a lot less frightening and much easier to understand.

> OBSIDIANA: "Mommy's proud of me! She thinks it's pretty cool. In the beginning she didn't really understand, and I remember her one time wanting to know where all this 'heathenism' came from. I think one of the things that caught her attention, that made her stop to see what it was all about, was a copy of *Ancient Ways* I had gotten. The illustrations were the first thing that caught her eye. She started looking, and she started reading little passages here and there, looking at some of the photographs, and that broke the ice."

Be Patient. If your talk isn't going well, and your family seems to be getting really upset, angry, or are reacting in some other really negative way, don't push it; it's better to politely change the subject. Arguing will not help your cause, and neither will storming out of the room. There will always be other chances.

Religious persecution can be subtle. And those who practice it, especially when they're your parents, don't believe they're doing anything wrong. This can be immensely confusing, since we all tend to expect unconditional love and acceptance from our families. The battle is a lot more clear-cut when it's between strangers—you know they are the "enemy" and can oppose them with a clear conscience. But being misunderstood by your own parents can be heartbreaking.

Things aren't going to change overnight. Besides having to overcome ways of thinking that have had years to develop, your family is going to have to learn a new way of looking at you, which takes time. They may have to make more adjustments than you can predict. For instance, the day after I appeared on the cover of our local newspaper in full ritual dress, my mother, an attorney, found herself having to act as a spokesperson for the Craft to half the coworkers she ran into in court that day. My younger brother had to endure a lot of teasing from his schoolmates about the fact that his sister was known around school as a Witch.

If you are able to help your family understand and accept your faith, while preserving a good relationship with them, you will have overcome one of the greatest challenges any Witch will ever face. If it is not possible for you, then accepting that will be your challenge.

Love and Marriage

In the early days of Gardnerian covens, you were only permitted to join if you are in a working partnership with another person of the opposite sex, who was also preferably your lover or spouse. There are still some groups that stick to this rule, but it has been mostly thrown out as unfair to singles, gays and lesbians, and people who are in an interfaith relationship.

Unfair as it is, the inspiration behind it is understandable. A primary focus of Witchcraft is the joining of the God and Goddess, the two different halves completing each other. It only requires a slightly wider focus to see that this doesn't have to be exclusionary. To achieve a successful, intimate relationship with another person—any other person—requires a lot of work and commitment. It is not only a great accomplishment, but also a magical act. No, of course you should not have to bring a partner to join a coven. But if you want to be fully and completely a Witch, you should do your best to cultivate healthy, emotionally intimate relationships with others.

Should Your Mate Be Wiccan?

There are many different viewpoints on interfaith relationships, from "no problem" to "no way," to anything in between. This is a subject about which I personally have done a lot of thinking, and I still don't have a definite answer. I have, however, come to the conclusion that *every* relationship is an interfaith relationship, to some extent, and should be treated as such. No two people worship exactly the same way, even within the same religion. This means that it's absolutely necessary to take for granted that you will have differences in philosophy, and remain openminded and respectful of those differences.

If your partner isn't Wiccan or Pagan, it helps if you have similar spiritual outlooks, and you can separate that from the methods by which you express your spirituality. Then you will be able to see past the trappings and semantics, and find the basic faith you have in common. If your religions are contradictory, it's more of a challenge. Try to find some common goals, values, and interests. It *is* possible for two people with very different philosophies to have a successful relationship—look at James Carville and Mary Matalin!

If you are not currently seeing anyone, you might want to take a moment to think about how important it is to you that your partner shares your tradition. Do you plan to be very active in the Pagan community? Is it important to you to have a Pagan household? Do you want to raise your children in the Craft? Or do you consider your relationship with the Gods to be very personal—unnecessary to share with anyone else? Are there other, more important things you would look for in a partner, such as a similar political outlook, parenting philosophy, hobbies and interests? In the end, of course, you can only sketch out the person who might be "right" for you. The Gods have their own plan, and their own ideas, and they will often surprise you.

MARGOT: "Emily [my wife] is trying to explore her Carribean roots. It's been hard, because her family is very assimilated, so they don't know a lot about the Orishas—about Puerto Rican culture, pre-Christianity. But that's not just her journey, that's my journey too. Because she's the person I want to share my life with, no journey she takes, even a spiritual test of the soul that she has to undertake alone, she isn't completely alone because a part of me goes with her."

Working Partnerships

A working partnership is a commitment between two people to do magic and ritual together. It is a much closer and intimate connection than just that of coven-mates. Working partners do not have to be lovers as well; they can be platonic friends or even siblings. The only requirements are that they get along very well, genuinely love and care about each other, and are committed to helping each other in their magical growth. The two can belong to a coven, to separate covens, or not belong to any at all—but their partnership is their first priority.

What are the benefits of having a working partner? It is a nice compromise between being solitary and being part of a coven. You will have a trusted friend with whom you can share your ideas and your magical workings. You can teach each other and learn from each other. If one of you is male and the other female, you will be embodying the polarity of the God and Goddess, and will balance each other out. If you are of the same gender, you can delve deeper into the Mysteries of that gender; and you will see yourself mirrored in your partner. You will be able to do more elaborate (but still manageable) rituals than you could do alone. And sometimes it's just nice to have company!

I recommend a working partnership as a transition between solitary and coven work. If your partner is more experienced than you, it can be an intensive teaching situation. If you are both at about the same stage of your magical development, you can learn together, screw up together, and laugh together! If you decide that you want to start working with larger groups, you will already know something about the energy and interpersonal dynamics between people in circle. In general, it's usually a great experience.

If your romantic partner is not Wiccan, and you want to form a magical partnership with someone else, go ahead—but be very careful. You will be sharing magic and ritual on a very deep and intimate level, and it can very easily draw your attention and energy away from your primary relationship. Also, Wicca is a very sexually driven tradition; if you do the Great Rite in Token properly, you will feel as if (on some level) you have just made love with your partner. Many people feel their bodies responding physically at the moment when the athame touches the bottom of the chal-

A magical partnership means a lot more than friendship.

ice. If your relationship with your significant other is sexually monogamous, you may feel yourself slipping a little—or being tempted to slip. Even if you are polyamorous, you'll still need to keep the focus on your primary partner. Remember your priorities.

Wiccan couples tend to do magic together, and often they also consider themselves magical partners. If you're fortunate enough to be in this kind of situation, great! Sharing the Craft can deepen a relationship, which in turn can affect your magical practice in positive ways.

Because so much of Wiccan magic and philosophy is built on the idea of the complement of opposites, making a relationship work can actually be one of the most spiritually rewarding tasks you can undertake. All the self-help books available would seem to prove this fact: People fall in love very easily, but they speak different languages—especially if one is male and the other female.

As far as Wicca is concerned, however, you are the two halves of the Whole, and you are finding your way back to each other. Your union is the most sacred thing in the Universe. Even if you are the same gender, you are still two separate people, with different ways of looking at the world, different hopes and fears. When you channel the force of your love into the strength you will need to make a relationship successful, you are doing serious magical work. A true partnership of love is one way of understanding the Gods on their deepest level.

If your partner is Wiccan, you are actually having two relationships at once: On one hand, you are the couple taking the dog for a walk and doing the dishes. On the other hand, you are High Priest and High Priestess of your circle, traveling between the worlds and working magic. Some have suggested that these two sides of your life should be kept separate; that they will only interfere with one another. But to the contrary, kept in balance, the two sides will help each other. Meditating together can help to give peace and clarity in the middle of a heated argument. And if you are giving each other what you need on an everyday basis, you will have a more fulfilling magical life. Just as the Gods are not only present when you are doing ritual, when you're doing something as "mundane" as watching TV together, you are still two magical beings.

Sex Magic

When people ask me what it feels like to raise and release a cone of power, I tell them they already know. "Have you ever had an orgasm?" I ask. Then they understand. Sex is one of the most powerful magics—if not *the* most powerful—there is. Human sexuality is a deep and ingrained part of the psyche, it is the way we come close to the Gods, it is about joining and creating.

In many ways, sex is one of the most important components of Nature religion; it is an act of the Gods because it is creative. It puts something into the world that was not there before. This does not mean that every sexual act must result in the literal conception of another being. Gay and lesbian sex, sex while using birth control, and sex that doesn't involve intercourse are all still sacred. When two people join in love, it is the symbolic union of the God and Goddess, which creates a new being of Unity. Even masturbation can be seen as a sacred act of self-love. There are ancient cultures whose creation myth involves a singular God ejaculating the universe.

There are Wiccans who take this as a reason for a polyamorous lifestyle, and some see it as a way to strengthen their monogamous relationship. Either way, it is unreasonable to require people to save themselves for their wedding day, or to expect everyone to be heterosexual. The idea of a holy person being forced into celibacy seems ridiculous to most Wiccans—why should the most spiritual people in our community be prohibited from expressing the basic life-force? (Neither does Wiccan philosophy, on the other hand, dictate that people *must* be sexually active!)

The energy you raise through sex magic can be used for workings, but it's best if you keep it purely celebratory at first. This way you can simply enjoy the new dimension to your lovemaking without having to think about focusing and sending the energy in any particular direction.

You already know how to set up sacred space for ritual. This follows the same principles. You *are* working magic; your goal here is to join in love with another person. Set up your space to work toward that goal. Keep in mind the lighting, the smells (incense is nice), the textures of the space you have chosen. It's no coincidence that people often light candles when preparing for a romantic evening. Candlelight has a soothing and mesmerizing effect on the mind. Collect a set of symbols for your altar, or just to keep in your mind, that will help your subconscious focus on your goal and your intent.

Before doing sex magic, take some time to breathe and focus together. Ground and center. It helps if you and your partner have discussed your feelings and your desires together beforehand. Don't speak if you don't have to. Take your lovemaking very slowly. Energy takes time to build up, and the longer you take, the more you will have to release in the end. Be aware of the rising and falling of each other's energy—and that of your energy together. When you hit a peak, give yourself over to it. When you feel one happening in your partner, join him. These energy peaks may or may not correspond with orgasms; there is a difference. Sex magic is very effective if you are able to have a simultaneous orgasm, but if worrying about achieving that is distracting you, drop the idea. It's not that important.

The most important part is not the mechanics but the intent. You are performing a sacred act, first and foremost. Approach your lovemaking with the same serenity and focus you would use for a ritual. Once you master that, the energy will become naturally high and easy to direct.

When you're comfortable enough to harness the energy of your sex magic for workings, wait until you have an appropriate need for a spell. You don't want to send the energy of an ecstatic orgasm in the direction of your frail grandpa who needs some gentle healing. Similarly, sex magic might not work well if you need to concentrate on a tough exam. Use it for workings that require a particularly passionate kind of energy, such as a self-healing, to break out of a bad habit or mood, to draw a new opportunity to you, for prosperity; and it can be especially useful if you're trying to conceive a child!

Set up sacred space and meditate together on the purpose of the spell. Make sure it's very clear in your mind, and that you are thinking the same thing. Keep it simple. "Prosperity" is a good one. "Getting a job close to home with good benefits and friendly coworkers in which I feel challenged and fulfilled" probably won't work. Remember, you are going to be focusing on this goal at a time when complex thoughts may be difficult. Make sure to ground and center.

Then, turn to each other and forget the purpose of the spell. Concentrate on your lovemaking as a powerful, magical, sacred act. Throw yourself into it completely. Be in the moment. Don't let yourself think about anything but what you are feeling right then.

Don't rush the buildup to orgasm. The longer you wait, the more powerful it will be (but you knew that already). When you come—and it's fine if that's at different times—let the image of your goal fill your mind. See the energy shooting off from you to do the job. Then relax and forget about it. A spell, once done, is less effective if you dwell on it. Enjoy a cuddle with your partner.

In the section on ritual, we touched on the subject of the Great Rite. This is the highest form of sex magic, because what was purely symbolic now becomes quite real and literal. When you and your partner make love, the two of you are acting out the roles of the God and Goddess. Now the God and Goddess are making love in the "roles" of humans; they are making love through you. Those who have experienced the Great Rite speak of it as one of the most intense of all magical experiences. It can be very carefully planned, or it can happen spontaneously.

Before you attempt the Great Rite, you should be comfortable with drawing down the moon or sun, and also with sex magic. Both techniques require a lot of concentration. Drawing down calls for a deep level of trance in which you become less aware of your body, and sex magic requires a deep level of trance in which you are fully and completely enthralled with your body and that of your partner. It would then stand to reason that the Great Rite in Truth is very tricky and something you should not rush. It also requires a good magical partnership and a deep level of trust. There are many people who have been practicing the Craft for several years and have never experienced a Great Rite in Truth. It is a gift from the Gods, and they decide whether or not to bestow it. We can plan and practice and meditate, but in the end, it is not entirely up to us.

It may seem a strange journey, to go from difficult discussions with your folks to the Great Rite in Truth in the space of the same chapter. But when you live magically, you will notice the boundaries between different parts of your life begin to dissolve—and you will see where the connections start. Love, whether it is between you and a lover or you and your mother, is still love. It is still a magical and sacred connection. And you are the same person—even though at times you may be a seductress and at other times someone's kid. As we notice the different faces we wear with different people, our relationships teach us what we need to learn about ourselves. In all these ways, we understand the relationship between the God and Goddess, and we come to know the Gods as faces of the One.

CHAPTER THIRTEEN

The Teenage Trip and College Life

JENNE: "I came out in the open in eleventh grade. Someone was doing a report on modern Witchcraft. It was so full of lies and inconsistency, I had to butt in and tell him what it was and what I believed. Once people knew I was a Pagan, I got my ass kicked. People used to call me 'bride of Satan.' They threw rocks at my head. I never denied that I was a Pagan, but I would never use the 'W' word till I got to college. It was so negative to me after everything that had happened, it took me a long time to reclaim the word."

If you're under eighteen, you may be interested in Witchcraft but don't know where to start. You may be reading a lot of books that contradict each other and raise more questions than they answer. If you're already practicing, you may be in a family that doesn't understand your beliefs or even opposes them. You may be faced with new challenges integrating the Craft into your school or social life. Faced with the necessity of being your own priest or priestess, you may wonder if you're doing things "right."

Many people come to the Craft while they're in their teens and still living with their parents. But these seekers face almost total disregard—from the books on the shelves written for adults, to the coven leader who says "Come back when you're eighteen." It doesn't seem to matter that there are thousands of young seekers out there who need good solid information; the fact is that they are still the legal dependents of their parents—and the parents of minors have the power to sue in their children's behalf. Wicca is still often equated with Satanism, and no author or coven leader wants to be accused of corrupting a minor.

> UGRIC: "When I started teaching years ago, I said I would not teach anyone under the age of eighteen. But as the years passed, I have had students as young as fifteen. When I started teaching minors, I got a lot of priests in my territory looking at me funny, saying, 'You're biting off a lot that you may not want, because you may get slapped with corrupting a minor and things like that.' The initial response to that was we decided to get the parents' permission. Well, that doesn't necessarily always work. Because the parents don't care about their kids. The kids are out there having sex, doing drugs, and yet if they get involved in something like this, [the parents] freak out. So I decided that I would teach my students to be responsible, do research, I would teach them to control their energy a little better. So I have no problem teaching minors."

Ugric is an exception to the rule. There are many young people learning the Craft entirely on their own. Adolescents often need to reject their parents' system of beliefs as they attempt to create their own separate identity. Since most people aren't being raised in Pagan homes, they must come to the Craft on their own, in answer to their own developing needs. Teenagers have the right to learn all their options, and to try them out to see what works for them.

To the Teenager

As a teen Witch, you have unique needs and concerns. It may seem at first as though everything is against you. Because you're underage, you can't get magical training. Your parents may not be supportive of your new path. And then there's the concern of being "out" in high school. It's ironic that what may be the ideal time to begin a magical life is also the most challenging time.

Practicing Wicca as a teenager may require a little extra ingenuity, but it's far from impossible.

Most Witches opt to discuss their chosen path with their parents at some point. As a teenager, the issue is a little more crucial for you. You don't have quite as much freedom or privacy as an independent adult, and although you may decide to keep your magical life to yourself, it might just not be possible.

Granted, parents can be understanding. But for most people, living as a Witch under their parents' roof is a ripe source for conflict. If your parents don't approve, you could be prohibited from having contact with your Wiccan friends or elders. Your parents may confiscate your books. You may find yourself being visited by the clergy of your parents' choice (so you can be saved), or even being sent into therapy to overcome this "problem" of yours. Think hard about how much you want to share with them.

If you choose to keep your practice a secret, you'll need some privacy; a safe place to keep your tools, supplies, and books; and somewhere to do ritual. But even if your parents have no objection to your practice, you still need your own space. Some parents think they have the right to walk into their children's rooms whenever they feel like it. At best, these intrusions will interfere with any spellwork you're doing or circles you have up. At worst, if your parents are opposed to your practice, they could start messing around with your magical tools and supplies. (A friend of mine had left candles burning for a spell, and her father "kindly" put them out for her.)

If privacy is an issue for you, have a talk with your parents about it. You needn't mention any specific reasons, just that it's important to you. You should have the right to your own space, no matter what. Do not yell, call names, or put them down. See if you can work out a system—a sign on the door that means "do not disturb," certain hours when you can get some alone time, or an understanding that if the door is closed, it means you are not open for business. This isn't just about Wiccan practice. Everyone needs a place to which they can escape once in a while.

Sometimes the straightforward approach doesn't work. However, anyone who follows a misunderstood and persecuted religion must learn to be resourceful. Sometimes doing outdoor rituals can solve them problem, or try visiting a Wiccan friend's house, or working around your parents' schedules.

In the spirit of compromise, try to eliminate possible trouble spots. My mother used to express her anxieties about my involvement in the Craft by constantly mentioning the safety risks of burning candles for my rituals and spells. Don't give them something to complain about—show that you know what you're doing by assuring them you will never leave a candle unattended. If you know they're unhappy with your magical practice, don't bring it up. You don't have to go so far as to hide all your books, just give them a low profile.

In the end, living as a Witch does not mean you must have an altar set up in your room or wear a pentacle. Live by the Wiccan philosophy, worship the Gods, work magic, and you will be a Witch. Your magic and your religion are private and personal, and you can always find space to do your work.

Wearing Your Pentacle to High School

If you're thinking about being out as a Witch in high school, be prepared; it is not easy. In a place where you may be taunted and shunned for dressing the wrong way, this unforgiving minisociety is often not averse to religious discrimination. When I made the decision to be public with my practice, I thought I had nothing left to lose. I was extremely unpopular all through my school years. I never really understood why, but by the time I got to high school I had given up trying. I was very excited about Wicca, and proud of my involvement, and I wanted to wear my pentacle. And, I thought, things couldn't possibly get worse.

I was wrong, of course. As soon as I said the 'W' word, there was trouble. People were keenly interested in the fact that I was a Witch, but no one wanted to hear any explanations. There were a few people—mostly teachers—who were familiar with Wicca, or at least were open-minded enough to ask intelligent questions. But mostly, it was hell.

Do I regret being out in high school? Yes, but only because I did it for the wrong reasons. I was still in that stage of my practice where I felt like I had to advertise what I was doing in order to feel legitimate. I wanted the pentacle around my neck as a label. My motivations were fuzzy. And so the hurt inflicted upon me by my classmates did a lot of damage.

Think about your motivations. Do you simply want to share this great thing you have found? Do you want to stand out in the crowd? Do you want to help foster public understanding of Wicca and Paganism? Do you simply see no reason why you should hide? Do you want to intimidate people? To be a "freak?" Is it that you have other friends who are Wiccan, and you want to belong to that group?

If you think your reasons are good, and you are prepared to deal with the consequences, then go for it. But you should exercise caution. If your goal is to show that Witches are just regular people and that Wicca is a legitimate religious path, don't wear black cloaks and huge silver pentacles all over your body. You might want to avoid the "W" word altogether. Understating your beliefs will make life easier for you in the long run. And if you are being harassed, remember that you can always go to your guidance counselor for help. She *should* be nonjudgmental.

The main problem is that if you decide being public isn't working out, you're still stuck there until you graduate. You really can't say, "I was just kidding about all that Witch stuff, ha ha." It's easy to come out of the closet. It is next to impossible to go back in.

How to Be a Teen in the Pagan Community

Although many covens exclude young people from membership, there are occasional exceptions. The High Priest or Priestess may decide that all they need is your parents' approval. But getting that may be difficult for you, if not impossible. Very rarely, a group will require absolutely no parental permission at all, but this is highly suspect. First of all, you should think twice about joining a coven without getting a reference from someone you trust—preferably from at least two people who don't know each other. Second, if a group is pleased to accept minors without talking to their folks, then you can assume they are (at best) ignorant, or (at worst) unconcerned with the law. If they won't cover their own butts, how can you be sure yours is safe?

It's possible to have a perfectly satisfying magical life without joining a coven. You can have companionship with your good friends, and you can communicate with the Gods directly, which is all that really matters. But what is missing is a sense of community. You may feel you are the only Witch in your town, or even your state.

No matter where you are, the community is there, so close you might trip over it. There are covens, workshops and activities, metaphysical stores, and even some public rituals in just about every major city outside of the Bible belt. And if you are in a particularly conservative area, there's always correspondence and the Internet. Here are a few ways you can get to know your Pagan neighbors and learn of the community without putting either yourself or them at risk:

1. GET A PEN PAL.   Most Wiccans, especially if one or both of you have a post office box, will feel comfortable corresponding. (I exchanged letters with a wonderful woman when I was in my teens, and I had the sense that I was under the care of an elder—even though I never actually saw her in person.) To find pen pals, look in the classified sections of New Age and Pagan magazines. *Circle Network News* has a great pen-pal service, the Pagan Spirit Alliance, and that was how, eight years ago, I met someone who is still one of my best friends.

2. JOIN A RELATED GROUP.   Many environmentalist groups, like Earth First! have a substantial Pagan membership. If you join one of these organizations, you can make contacts and you'll be doing the Mother Earth a lot of good, as well—something that can hardly be objectionable to your parents. Also, the Unitarian Universalist Society has a subgroup called CUUPS, or Covenant of Unitarian Universalist Pagans. And the Society for Creative Anachronism, or SCA, is a medieval reenactment organization that has a very prominent Wiccan/Pagan membership. These groups are national, fairly easy to find, and you should have no problem getting hooked up with one of their chapters.

3. GO TO A "PAGAN WAY" GROUP.   Many Wiccan and metaphysical bookstores have Pagan Way or "Wicca 101" classes that you can join, usually in exchange for a food contribution or a small weekly fee. Some of them might not accept minors, but it can't hurt to ask. Since the classes in religious education take place in a public shop, attending one isn't as risky as joining a coven. If you have been studying and doing ritual on your own for a couple of years already, you may think a class would be a waste of time. I recommend that you go anyway, because it will give you the chance to meet the Wiccans in your area and to get a sense of the community around you. You may meet some people your own age; you may connect with future coven members—who knows?

Just try not to be too starry-eyed. Remember: The fact that someone has been in the Craft longer than you also means they've had more opportunity to screw up.

4. START YOUR OWN GROUP.   Obviously, this is not something to jump into right away. Being a group leader, even if it's just for a discussion group, is hard work and requires some experience. But if you have a friend or two who are interested in the Craft, and you've been studying long enough so that you think you are ready, plan a regular meeting time. If you think you are ready and you really aren't, the Gods will point this out to you rather forcefully. The best format for a new exploratory group would be that of a forum for discussion and study. Plan topics for discussion, do exercises like those found in this book, meditate, celebrate the sabbats together, and so on. It's not a good idea to place a heavy emphasis on ritual in the beginning. If you want to try ritual as part of your group activity, keep it simple.

The Craft at College

BLAIR: "There is special-interest housing at this college. The one dorm that is big for special interests is Demarest. They have housing for Hebrew sections, lesbigaybisexual—it's a very diverse housing and it's meant to be that. They do not tolerate any biases. You always see Jewish people gathering together on Fridays to have their own small services. Well, there are a couple of Pagans that are there now. And we've already decided that because it's so diverse, we plan on getting together. Thing is, they don't care if you walk around with no clothes on, in that dorm, sometimes. If there's any faculty there, they tell you, 'please, become decent,' but they are extremely open-minded. So it's friendly to about everyone."

Collegiate Pagans are coming out of the woodwork. At many major colleges and universities, Pagan student groups are prominently involved with the college community. It's no surprise that the signs of a growing religion should be so evident in this section of the population—it has always been young people who grab onto trends and promote them.

After the age of eighteen, you can start to go coven-shopping, if that's what you want. But you need not look very far—there may be a group or two right on campus, or you can form your own there.

JENNE: "My first year [at Drew], after I learned how to play around on the Internet and the campus-wide information system, I sent around a message for all those interested in Paganism and Nature spirituality . . . and that's how PAN, Pagan Awareness Network, was formed."

You may think that it would be better to train with an older, more experienced crowd. But you can learn a lot from your mistakes, and those of your fellow students, when you practice in a college group. You may fumble along, but when it works, it will work beautifully.

How do you go about finding a Pagan group on your college campus? If there is an officially recognized Pagan student organization, you'll find it listed in any directory of student groups. If the college is particularly hip, the Pagan group will be in the chaplain's directory of religious groups. If not, it'll be in the general listing of campus organizations. The group may also have flyers posted, informing students of their open circles and meeting times.

If you decide to form a group of your own, there are many ways to go about finding other interested people. Place an ad in the college newspaper. Check out the bulletin board at the nearest metaphysical bookstore. Put up flyers around campus, check the classified ads in Pagan magazines.

Since groups of this kind tend to form in organic ways, you won't need to worry too much about the number of people or whether the group has a specific direction, at least in the very beginning. People who need to find each other, will. It seems that the most stable covens often have started out as a group of friends, so don't exert too much authority over your group as it forms.

Once you have got a pretty consistent membership, you can decide whether you want to become an official campus group. This will mean different things in different schools. In some places, you'll get the use of an office in the student center, in others, you'll receive funding for supplies and operating costs, and in some schools you'll just be given a space to hold your meetings. You will, of course, need to apply to the student council in order to be "official"; this usually just means proving that there is a genuine need on your campus for a Pagan student group. You're going to be asserting that there are several students who would want to be members of such a group, and you're going to be explaining ways in which your group will serve the student body as a whole. You may be required to collect signatures on a petition, and possibly to stand up in front of the student council and give a presentation.

There are pros and cons to all of this. Obviously, if you're going to be the leader of a Pagan Student Union, you're going to be out of the broom closet. In fact, even just joining such a group limits your anonymity—anyone can come to meetings and see who's there. You'll also have to deal with campus bureaucracy, paperwork, and lots of seemingly useless rules.

However, as an official campus organization, your group will have more power and presence. If you are at all concerned about the public's view of Wicca, you will be in a position to do a lot of advocacy work. Along with those basic things like meeting space and access to a copying machine, will come visibility. Anyone browsing down a list of campus organizations will see your group and perhaps will want to know more. At events where the student groups have information booths, you can offer pamphlets on Wicca. And you will be able to participate in campus events, community service, and even interfaith ceremonies, alongside other religious groups.

All this public presence doesn't come without a price. You must decide whether you are willing to risk possible harassment, and whether you are ready to answer the constant (and often annoying) questions about the Craft, when you decide to be a visible campus Pagan. And you may bring on a couple of well-meaning Christians in the business of saving souls. On a larger scale, the day a Pagan Student Union is formed, all the evangelical Christian groups on campus will tend to perk up their heads and gear up for battle.

If you are willing to face that sort of challenge, and if you believe it would be worth it for the privilege of being an official campus organization, go for it. Just make sure you are well-prepared. Before you apply to become part of the student union, have a series of meetings to develop a coherent set of goals for your group. Will you meet every week? What will you do at your meetings? Will you have workshops? Open circles? Will you get involved with the other religious organizations on campus? Will you do any charity work? (Deciding in favor of this last one, besides being important anyway, will help to improve the image many people have of Pagans and Witches.)

You might also want to locate a large Wiccan or Pagan church to sponsor you. Covenant of the Goddess, while mostly a union of independent covens, does include the occasional student group. Aligning yourself with a legal church, and being under the counsel of an elder or two, will add to your legitimacy in the eyes of the student government. And the guidance you'll get can be extremely helpful. It will probably be harder to get into CoG than it will be to get into student government, but it will be worth the trouble.

Let's say you are not interested in joining or forming an official student group; you want a group to learn with and worship with, but no connection to your school. Maybe you think your student council is a joke, you don't like the current student group, you want to keep your practice more private, or maybe you just don't want to deal with the bureaucracy. In such cases, you may be able to find private circles and study groups that are already up and running. If you don't find any, start your own. Hunt out the other Pagans on campus. You can also see if there's anyone in a current Pagan student group who wants to try something more intimate and less official.

The recommended guidelines for running a Pagan student group are pretty much the same for running any other kind of Pagan group. Allow the group to choose its own direction, but keep a focus. Encourage participation, keep learning and celebrating! There is one main trap into which many Pagan student groups fall: The leader (or leaders) wind up doing all the work. If that leader happens to be you, don't let that even start to happen. Delegate, delegate, and delegate. And don't be too attached to your status as leader. If you want supreme authority, you will also have supreme responsibility. And your group will turn into a cult of personality—a direct contradiction to the Wiccan philosophy in which everyone is clergy. Responsibilities should be shouldered equally by all the active members.

If you are practicing solitary, you don't have to worry too much about meeting space. You'll only need to negotiate time and privacy with your roommate or housemates, so you can do your circles and meditations undisturbed. But if you have a group, where are you going to meet? Back home your bedroom served fine for a temple, but it's not comfy to try to squeeze ten people into a dorm room.

Depending on your school, you may be allowed to use a room in the student center. This will serve well for regular meetings in which you have discussion and study going on, but it might not be appropriate for ritual. Even assuming you can cover up the windows on the door for privacy, do you want to be walking down the hallway in your ritual robe and run into a bunch of frat boys?

You may be able to meet at the house of someone who lives off campus (yours, if you're so fortunate). If you're blessed with a large communal living room, all you have to do is find a day and time when your housemates can vacate the space. This is an ideal situation, since you won't be restricted by the college's rules and regulations at all.

Can your college really place limits on your religious life? Yes, if it includes doing something that is already against the rules. For instance, in a lot of dorms, it is "illegal" to burn candles, since doing so is considered a fire hazard. You may be able to get special permission, you may not. In my old school, because it was a state college, we were not supposed to hold "religious services" in our dorm rooms. We understood the reasoning—separation of church and state—but it wasn't as if we could just go over to the official "campus Pagan temple" instead!

> BLAIR: "Rutgers [University] totally and absolutely prohibits candle-burning, incense-burning, any kind of flames, smoking of any nature in the hallways. They permit it loosely in dorm rooms as long as it is not to excess, and if nothing can be smelled outside of the door. And it is one of the only policies they enforce. It does not matter if it's for religious purposes."

One of the simplest solutions to these hassles: Go outside. Many colleges and universities have athletic fields that are quite deserted at night. Aside from the odd drunken reveler or amorous couple, you will be able to perform your rituals in peace. Just be aware that if you have a bonfire you could get in trouble with campus cops, or at the very least, you might be more visible than you want to be. It's one thing to do circle in a semipublic place, it's another entirely to start advertising.

> LAUREL: "I changed my religous 'bent' in college, and here I was a church-music major. Nobody knew during the first year that I was Wiccan. Then a couple of students on campus were curious about the New Age community, and since I had already been doing that for a while, I took them to classes and such, but they noticed that I tended to hang with a slightly different crew once in a while. Then they noticed that the people I was hanging with were wearing pentacles. Then they finally realized that I was too—it was just on a long

chain. Finally, in my second year, somebody asked me about it, and I said that I was Wiccan."

As usual, the harder path is the more rewarding. Those who were lucky enough to find the Craft at such a young age are given a head start of sorts. But those who are stubborn enough to continue their Craft studies in the face of all the hassles are the truly dedicated ones.

CHAPTER FOURTEEN

Speaking for the Craft

MISHA: "This past summer I went to Lithuania to participate in a festival and symposium on the recreation of the folk and specific Pagan traditions of the pre-Baltic peoples. Lithuania was the last Eastern European country to be Christianized, and there are those in Lithuania who are hoping that now is a good time to go back.

"I wound up on the festival grounds, some 150 miles north of Vilnius, as the only American in the festival and the only American that anybody there had ever seen. One of the most interesting moments was when they asked me to give a talk on the contemporary state of American Paganism. I had to assure them that I was, in fact, no expert on American Paganism. I was only there because I had two weeks off from work and a plane ticket. Giving the talk proved somewhat difficult. There were two common languages among the participants: Russian, spoken by the Poles, Latvians and Lithuanians; and English, for the Finns, Germans, and me. Fortunately, I used to live in Russia and spoke the language reasonably well, so I wound up giving my speech in Russian and then translating it into English for the Finns and Germans. The people I was speaking to didn't know the first thing about the contemporary state of American Paganism, and I could have told them that there were 750,000 of us who all took off alternate Thursdays to dance widdershins around a large lump of cheese. I did the best I could. It was received well enough that I lived to tell the tale, although I don't think any kind of pedagogic history was made that afternoon."

VICTORIA: "In terms of the future, I see Wicca becoming more generally accepted and more generally understood. I don't think everyone has to be 100 percent out of the 'broom closet,' but to whatever degree one is comfortable doing that, I think it's necessary. We need to educate ourselves about other religions and the history of Wicca to have an intelligent discourse with other people about it. We need to be educators in a gentle way."

You don't have to go on talk shows, write books, or own a magical shop to be a public Witch. Telling your coworkers, wearing a pentacle, having magical books on your shelves, or even browsing in one of those shops can, to some extent, declare your identity to the world—and the world in general will probably think you're a Satanist.

For this reason, many Wiccans choose to keep their practice as privileged information, shared only with family and close friends—sometimes only with fellow coven members. It is important to think seriously about whether or not you're going to be public.

Certainly there are numerous pamphlets and books available on the Craft; accurate information is available for those who want it. But that may not be much help when your ex-spouse is trying to take custody of your children.

KERRI: "It can be dangerous to tell the wrong people what your religious beliefs are. Unfortunately, the burning times are not over. It's good when you tell people about your religion because it shows that there are more of us than people think, and it can also help in changing misconceptions about the religion. But at the same time it sets you up to be a victim. People will use it against you. And the courts don't necessarily uphold the Constitution."

If you decide that you can afford to be open about your religion, great. The more people there are who identify themselves as Pagan, the sooner the misunderstandings will stop. This is for a couple of reasons: First, there will be more sources of accurate information to effectively counter the Satanist/loony propaganda. People will be able to say either that they themselves are Wiccan—or at least that they have a close friend who is—and they know what it really means. The same way negative stereotypes are spread, so the positive ones can be: by word of mouth. This can also work in more subtle ways. Folks will begin to notice that perfectly ordinary people are wearing pentacles. This is the same guy you see in the supermarket, the same woman you work with, the same little girl who's on your daughter's soccer team.

It is a shame that so far, many of those who are willing to be open about their practice are also those who are very eccentric. This perpetuates the idea that Wicca is a fringe religion. One expects to see a pentacle on someone with green hair and black fingernails. Not that there's anything wrong with personal expression, but once those who dress more conservatively start quietly affirming their religion—once someone's grandma wears *her* pentacle—then the image of Wicca can more quickly change in a positive way.

> DAVID: "As Pagans, we have a great responsibility to project ourselves as positive, caring, intelligent people whose behavior should be emulated. Every time I wear my pentacle in public, I realize that my actions and words are the impressions that people will carry with them, and will be what they associate with the symbol of my faith. One of the most sincere compliments I ever received was when a friend said to me, 'Well, Dave, if *you* believe in all this Witchcraft stuff, then I guess it can't be all bad.' "

The main goal of advocacy for the Craft is not to be liked, but simply to be *understood*. When people give me a hard time about being a Satanist, my reaction is, "Hate me if you like, but at least understand what you're hating me for!" Although a lot of people would love to see the world become Pagan, it is not our work to make that happen. I have never met a Wiccan or Pagan who went around proselytizing. We do not care if people agree with our views, but we do want them to know what those views are.

In the Wiccan philosophy, where the magical and the mundane are intertwined, being forced into the "broom closet" means being unable to worship and celebrate fully and completely. The Craft is an even more important aspect of a Witch's life than her occupation—that can be left behind at the office. She is a Witch twenty-four hours a day. Wicca is not a hobby or an interest, it is a way of life. And yet we sometimes may feel forced to keep it under wraps.

This is not about being pushy; we do not need to wear a pentacle or shout "I am a Witch!" from the rooftops. No, you don't *have* to tell anyone that you're Wiccan; but wouldn't it be nice to have the choice? Advocacy means helping to make sure that we do not have to apologize for what we are and what we believe.

There are many different ways you can work toward better public understanding of the Craft—and not all of them involve being "out" yourself. These can include:

1. WEAR A PENTACLE.   Or if you like, an ankh, Isis, Goddess pendant, labyrinth, medicine wheel, or any symbol that effectively represents what you believe. This will not only help you to find other Pagans, but will also prompt questions from the curious. If you wear a pentacle, you know that not all the reactions will be polite—often they may consist of nothing but a nervous stare. Many people still think a pentacle is a symbol of Satanism. Some Satanists do use it; but so do Wiccans, and we are in the vast majority. (Don't tell people that as long as it is right-side-up, it is "good," because some Wiccan traditions use it inverted at times.)

The fact is, we are not concerned with what Satanists do or who they are. We use a pentacle as a symbol of our faith, and that's the end of it. You may wish to skip the risk and wear something more innocuous, like an ankh. But the pentacle is the one symbol that is used pretty much universally by Wiccans; so it serves to identify you as part of the larger group—and therefore does good for the group as a whole.

2. Don't attempt to hide your beliefs.   This is different from going out of your way to talk about them, which may not be appropriate. Simply act as though Wicca were as ordinary a religion as the one your neighbors practice. Observe the sabbats, ask for time off to go to festivals, keep your magical things displayed with pride in your home. If you try to keep your practice a secret and are then discovered, people may think a Wiccan practice is something worth hiding—that it involves something immoral or illegal. If you act as though you are proud of your tradition (which I hope you are), others will perceive your pride.

There are, of course, different degrees to which you can be open about your practice and your beliefs. You don't have to post it on a billboard. You may choose to tell your close friends, but not your conservative coworkers. Just make sure the two groups don't mix, and be aware of the risk (however small) that they will. And you don't have to use the word Witch or Pagan, in order to live as one. There are many symbols, particularly Goddess-symbols and Native American ones, that you can feel free to wear or display without having people think you're a Satanist. You may not be identifying yourself completely with Wicca, but you will still be promoting understanding of a natural, magical, and myth-based lifestyle—which is helpful in itself.

3. Write a letter to the editor.   If you see an article in a newspaper or magazine that casts Witches in a negative light, or promotes inaccurate information about one of the holidays, write in (anonymously, if that's more comfortable for you).

> Obsidiana: "[One] week in Ann Landers, a Wiccan 'minister' wrote an objection to Ann calling a woman a 'witch,' and he wrote about what Witches really are. She said she apologized, but in her original copy, the word began with a *b* and it was her editor that changed it!"

Likewise, if a television program supposedly about witches pisses you off, write to the network. This kind of response can really make a difference.

4. Join, or give to, an advocacy group.   Numerous organizations exist all over the country that are specifically meant to change the image of Witches in American society. This includes

the Witches' Anti-Discrimination Lobby, the Lady Liberty League (through Circle Sanctuary), and the Witches League for Public Awareness (out of Salem, Massachusetts). Groups like the Covenant of the Goddess, the Earthspirit Community, and the Church of All Worlds also do a great deal of advocacy work. You can donate your time, energy, or money to help them along—and this, again, can be done anonymously. If you are a lawyer, your donated services can be especially helpful, because many of these groups get involved in religious discrimination lawsuits and need Wiccan-friendly representation.

5. GET INTO THE MEDIA.   This, of course, isn't for everybody. You have to be in a place in your life where you can afford to be known as a Witch, you have to be very well-spoken, and you have to possess a pretty tough exterior.

If you want to go that way, there are a number of things you can do. Write a short letter about yourself and about Wicca and send it to your local newspaper as an idea for a story. I did this one Halloween, figuring that the paper would find it an amusing little seasonal feature. I ended up on the front page in full color (Westchester County, New York's *Herald Statesman*, October 28, 1991). The next year, about the same time, I received a call from *Good Day New York,* a morning news program. They had seen the article and wanted to do a feature on me and my partner. Soon after the airing of the TV show, my local paper in New Jersey called me for an interview. You don't have to let your fame snow-ball like this—it leads to a lot of work. Nevertheless, I had a lot of fun, and the excitement did eventually die down.

You might think it's hard for someone with little experience in the Craft to get much media time. But because of the general public's misunderstanding, all you have to do is identify yourself as a Witch, and many members of the media will assume you're an expert. The way they see it, either Witchcraft is something you're born with (like a talent for music), or else it's just another religion like Christianity. The idea of an initiatory path, or a religion in which everyone is clergy, is totally foreign to most people. So even if you've only been practicing for a year or two, you're probably still a full-fledged Witch to them, and, as such, a fascinating subject for an interview. If you think you know your stuff, go for it.

Keep in mind that there are risks. Not everyone who wants to interview you will have your best interests in mind, or will be as concerned with accuracy as with amusing the public. Take commonsense precautions and use your intuition when talking to someone from a newspaper or TV show. If you feel that a reporter is aiming for a sensationalistic angle in the story, don't attempt to change it, just politely decline to participate.

When it comes time for the interview, dress normally and avoid giving any openings for misunderstandings. In other words, you can discuss Wicca accurately and openly without bringing your athame, mentioning that you work skyclad, talking about ritual sex, and so forth. Of course there's no way you can predict everything. Just be as cautious as possible.

This kind of attitude can really turn the tables on the sensationalistic interviewers. One of the funniest moments I can recall is when Laura, a representative from the Covenant of the Goddess, was being interviewed by Gordon Elliott on *Good Day New York*. It was part of the same Halloween broadcast I was on, except while my segment was taped, hers was done live. The producers chose to hold Laura's interview at the Limelight, a Gothic dance club in New York City. The club was decorated to the hilt for Halloween, complete with spiderwebs and spooky sound effects. Laura had come to the interview in a very tasteful navy blue suit, complete with a white ruffled blouse and a tiny silver pentacle pendant.

As the interview progressed, there were screams and demonic laughter in the background, the cameraman was shooting on all kinds of weird angles, and Gordon Elliott looked more and more ridiculous in his sparkly wizard costume. Laura was obviously the only sane one in the place. After a few minutes of her calm and educated answers to his silly questions, Gordon Elliott actually got serious—realizing that this was no joke, and that Witches were worth talking to.

Being a public Witch is a real challenge, but those who have the strength to do it are definitely appreciated.

Speaking for the Craft

JUDY: "For me, the important part of Wicca is that we see the sacredness of Nature, of Mother Earth. She is in deep trouble and needs healers and advocates, and, of course, our survival is entirely dependent on Hers. I would hope that we can bring this Earth-oriented perspective into the general religious "conversation" that is always going on. Just as the Quakers have always been a minority, but a respected one, and for three hundred years they have been a consistent voice for peace and social justice—I would hope that we could be the same kind of consistent and respected voice for ecological sanity."

If you do decide to be open about your beliefs, you will find yourself continually put into the position of Official Spokesperson for the Entire Neo-Pagan Movement. People just don't have a clue, and when you say you're Wiccan (or a Witch, or Pagan), the question, "What does that mean?" will naturally follow. And that's the best you can hope for. Otherwise they'll be making up their own answers, which probably won't be very flattering.

Wicca is a pretty complex religion, and it isn't easy to sum it up in the space of a coffee break. Furthermore, even if you did have the time, most people don't want to hear the entire history of Paganism, starting with the Stone Age and going up through Gerald Gardner to the present day. They just want a basic idea of what it's about.

I made this mistake one day when someone looked at my pentacle and asked me what it meant. I gave a discourse on the history and meaning of the symbol, with many different possible interpretations: the four elements plus spirit with the circle unifying them all, the image of a human body with arms outstretched, the "endless knot" of Arthurian legend, and so on, ad nauseum. When I wound down, the guy looked at me and said, "Yes, but what does it *mean*?" I said, "Oh, it means I'm a Witch." He smiled and said, "Oh!" That was all he wanted to know. I had definitely overdone it.

One-liners

The first step is to come up with a brief description of Wicca that isn't too scholarly or threatening, but which you still feel is accurate. This shouldn't be any longer than one or two sentences.

If the individual wants to know more, he'll ask. Here are some examples of ones I've used:

- "It's a revival of pre-Christian European Nature religion."
- "You're familiar with Native American religion? It's the European equivalent."
- "It's a magical, celebratory, Nature religion."

LAUREL: "According to the questions they ask, you can tell whether they really want to know or not. I would give them my standard definition: I would say I belong to a polytheistic nonprosletyzing, life-affirming, Earth-based religion. Now, if they were serious they would pursue each phrase, and I would explain further. If not, they'd go, 'Oh,' and not pursue it. That works great with Jehovah's Witnesses."

EXERCISE: Role-play

Find a friend to do this with, or, if you're alone, you can write it out, talk it out, or use a mirror. Pretend that one of you knows nothing about Wicca and has just learned that the other is a Witch. Take turns asking questions and coming up with realistic answers.

1. Ask some intelligent questions, such as: What do you believe? What is your idea of God? Where do you worship?
2. Ask some less intelligent questions, such as: Isn't that evil? Can you turn me into a toad? Do you fly?
3. Ask some challenging questions, such as: Do you know you're going to Hell? What kind of a stupid religion is this? Do you know Jesus loves you?

   You'll notice that most of the questions, when answered, will lead to more. Keep the conversation going until it reaches a natural conclusion. You'll find this exercise extremely useful when you are asked these questions in real life. Even if you don't plan to be public about your practice, you never know when you might be accidentally "outed," and it helps to be prepared—so it's not any more of a disaster than it has to be.

Sometimes you'll be asked questions that indicate sincere interest. If your questioner really wants to know more, just explain as best you can. Some questioners won't be taking you seriously. If they are giving you a hard time, don't play along—just end the conversation. Most people will wake up and notice that you're not making a joke and will either ask a real question or let the subject drop.

Then there are those who deserve a category all to themselves: those helpful types who want to tell you the Truth about Jesus and how He loves you. And who want to warn you that you are going to burn in Hell unless you change your ways. Sometimes you can get prepared, such as when well-dressed folks with brief-cases are ringing your doorbell on a Sunday afternoon. Other times, you may be caught completely off-guard—you had no idea this distant cousin you're chatting with at a wedding reception was a born-again Christian, and now she's pulled out her Bible and shows no signs of retreat.

First, try to see it from their perspective. They sincerely believe that you're in for an eternity of suffering, and they're trying to help you out. To "save" you.

Second, stay polite. If you have told the person that you're Wiccan, you are now a representative for the entire Neo-Pagan community. Even a conversation on such a small scale really does make a difference in how the world views the Craft. That means that saying things like "Someday the past two thousand years will be looked upon as 'the Christian interlude,' " or "My Goddess can beat up your God" would be a bad idea. Even if someone else's path isn't the right one for you, it may be exactly right for them—and you have no business judging.

Third, don't get pulled into a heated theological discussion, unless you like being frustrated and have a lot of time to kill. It can be tempting to point out inconsistencies in logic and to dazzle with your knowledge of the history of religion, but try to resist the urge. First of all, it's not nice to your Bible-thumping com-panion—and besides, the past experience of many people has determined that you're not going to win anyway.

So what do you do? Politely thank your potential savior for her concern and interest, but state with a smile that you're quite happy with your own religion. That will usually be the end of the conversation. If not, refer back to steps one through three and then repeat yourself.

Most Witches have at least one funny story to tell about their encounters with well-meaning Christians. I am no exception. A few years ago, my college friends and I had just finished setting up for our Samhain circle when there came a knock on the door. These Jehovah's Witnesses took one look at the altar and turned right around. I guess they figured we were beyond the scope of their influence.

It is important to keep a sense of humor in these situations. There is only so much we can do, and I believe one of the reasons Wicca will endure is our refusal to take ourselves too seriously.

> MEILIKKI: "My friend gets all bent out of shape because on Halloween they do the Witches with the green faces and long noses and warts, and she's like, 'We're not like that!' And I'm like, 'Give me a break, you gotta be able to laugh at yourself.' I even think it's funny when they call us a bunch of tree huggers."

Most of us don't have the luxury of living in a tumbledown cottage on the side of a mountain, where we can do skyclad rituals in our backyard and no one knows or cares that we're Wiccan. Most of us live in the real world, in apartment buildings where neighbors can smell the incense we burn, in neighborhoods where the

Witches and Pagans at a Pro-Choice rally in Washington, D.C.

Avon Lady sees our magical books. We go to schools where the other students will ask about the pentacle pendant; we work in offices where the boss will want to know why we need those specific eight days off every year. Subtlety is great, but it's damn near impossible to hide a magical practice completely.

So, one question inevitably leads to another, and there are probably many of us who came out of the "broom closet" whether we wanted to or not. I suggest that we make it a conscious choice. The only reason it's so hard to be publicly Wiccan in our society is misunderstanding. The only way that can be changed is by making information available to those who want it. There will always be Christians who try to convert people of other faiths. That's the least of our worries. We want to keep our jobs and keep custody of our children.

The smallest thing you can do toward advocacy is still worth doing. If you can't be open yourself—and there are plenty of legitimate reasons for that—then find ways to help anonymously. If you can just tell a friend or two, there will be two more people in the world who are friends with a Witch—and they will speak for us.

The ecstasy of the Craft is in the here-and-now. It is not about secrecy or separation. The greatest work we can do as Witches is to help bring magic into the mundane. Anything you can do to help people live magical lives without fear or shame will be a sacred act of transformation.

Conclusion: The Path Ahead

If you feel that you want to study and possibly practice the Craft, take a look at the recommended reading list that follows. It's important to get different viewpoints on the same subject. Even if you agreed with everything I said (which I would find hard to believe), another author will give you a new perspective, and maybe you'll change your opinion. It's also worthwhile to read about related subjects such as energy work, meditation, and myth. All these fields of study will enrich your practice of the Craft. Pick one or two titles that sound interesting and look for them at your local bookstore, or order them there.

If you've had enough reading for the time being, you can take a more basic route. Meditate. Go for walks outside. Surround yourself with wilderness, or look for the magic within the man-made world. Work magic. Listen to your dreams. Being a Witch does not mean stuffing the most information into your head; it means being able to truly connect with Deity on a basic level. And sometimes books can actually take you away from that goal.

Yes, more and more contradictions! As you know by now, Witchcraft is not a simple or easy path. But it can be extremely rewarding. As you open yourself up to the energy currents that flow through all things, as you allow yourself to see Deity in every being you come across, as you start to use all your senses, as you celebrate the simple changes in the seasons—you will find yourself living more completely than you did before. And you didn't even know you were missing anything.

Again, I urge you to go beyond this book. This is the beginning, not the end, of your spiritual journey. And although you can learn from books and from other people, the only true authority is the voice of the Gods. All the knowledge you can gather on this Earth is meant for only one thing: to allow you to hear that voice.

Appendix of Resources

Once you pick up one Pagan magazine, get involved with one church or organization, or do a search on the Web for *Wicca*, you will have amazing amounts of information at your disposal. The following isn't meant to be an exhaustive list—quite the contrary. It's just a starting point. I have included only resources that I have personally found to be of high quality, or that have been recommended to me by people I trust. No doubt there are hundreds more that are just as valuable.

Pagan Churches and Organizations

Church of All Worlds
P.O. Box 1542
Ukiah, CA 95482–1542

A Pagan group based on the spiritual teachings from Robert Heinlein's *Stranger in a Strange Land*.

Circle Sanctuary
(also includes the Lady Liberty League, a Pagan advocacy group,
and Circle Network News, a quarterly publication)
P.O. Box 219
Mount Horeb, WI 53572
(608) 924–2216
e-mail: circle@mhtc.net

Covenant of the Goddess
P.O. Box 1226
Berkeley, CA 94704

A legally recognized Wiccan church. Chapters nationwide.

The Earthspirit Community
P.O. Box 365
Medford, Massachusetts 02155
(617) 395–1023
e-mail: earthspirit@earthspirit.com

Advocacy Groups

Witches' Anti-Defamation League
Silver RavenWolf, director
P.O. Box 1392
Mechanicsburg, PA 17055–1392

Witches' League for Public Awareness
P.O. Box 8736
Salem, MA 01971–8736

Magazines

Connections
1705 14th St., Number 181
Boulder, CO 80302

Enchante: The Journal for the Urbane Pagan
John Yohalem
P.O. Box 735
New York, NY 10014–0735
(212) 691-0862
e-mail: enchante@escape.com

One of the best sources for Pagan satire.

Green Egg
P.O. Box 1542
Ukiah, CA 95482

Published by the Church of All Worlds (see listing under Churches
and Organizations)

Mezlim
P.O. Box 19566
Cincinnati, OH 45219

Occult Suppliers

Abyss Distribution
48–CEN Chester Road
Chester, MA 01011
(413) 623–2155

White Light Pentacles/Sacred Spirit Products
P.O. Box 8163
Salem, Massachusetts 01971–8163

Pagan Festivals

Rites of Spring (Memorial Day Weekend)
Twilight Covening (Columbus Day Weekend)
P.O. Box 502
Medford, MA 02155
(617) 395–1023
Run by the Earthspirit Community

Starwood (end of July)
Association for Consciousness Exploration
1643 Lee Road Number 9
Cleveland Heights, OH 44118

Pagan Spirit Gathering (June)
Circle Sanctuary
P.O. Box 219
Mount Horeb, WI 53572
(608) 924–2216

Web Sites

The NeoPagan Archive (lots of information about specific traditions)
http://www.lysator.liu.se/religion/neopagan/

Covenant of the Goddess (national Wiccan church)
http://www.cog.org/

The Earthspirit Community (information about ESC's activities and
general Wiccan/Pagan stuff)
http://www.earthspirit.com

Witchworlds
http://www.sfo.com/~wholebody/witchworlds.html (a veritable Wiccan/Pagan cornucopia)

Pagan Pathways
http://www.alt.net/~waltj/shea/paganp.html (more links than you could shake a wand at)

Recommended Books for Further Reading

I've read most of the books on this list and can recommend them without reservation. The rest have been recommended to me by people I trust. All are currently in print (except where noted), but some will be easier to find than others.

Chapter 1, Beginnings

Note: Most of these authors have also written other books, all of which are good.

Margot Adler, *Drawing Down the Moon*. Boston: Beacon Press, 1987.
Scott Cunningham, *Wicca: A Guide for the Solitary Practitioner*. St. Paul, MN: Llewellyn Publications, 1988.
Janet and Stewart Farrar, *What Witches Do*. Custer, WA: Phoenix Publishing Inc., 1983.
Starhawk, *The Spiral Dance*. New York: HarperCollins, 1989.
Doreen Valiente, *Witchcraft for Tomorrow*. Custer, WA: Phoenix Publishing Inc., 1989.

Chapter 2, Energy Work and the Elements

Barbara Ann Brennan, *Hands of Light: A Guide to Healing Through the Human Energy Field*. New York: Bantam New Age Books, 1987.

Chapter 3, Deity

Anything by Joseph Campbell.
Janet and Stewart Farrar, *The Witches' God*. Custer, WA: Phoenix Publishing Inc., 1989 and *The Witches' Goddess*. Custer, WA: Phoenix Publishing Inc., 1987.
Alan Richardson, *Earth God Rising: The Return of the Male Mysteries*. St. Paul, MN: Llewellyn Publications, 1990.

Chapter 4, Magic

Janet and Stewart Farrar, *Spells and How they Work* Custer, WA: Phoenix Publishing Inc., 1990.

Chapter 5, The Sabbats

Janice Broch and Veronica MacLer, *Seasonal Dance*. York Beach, ME: Samuel Weiser, Inc., 1993.

Pauline and Dan Campanelli, *Ancient Ways: Reclaiming Pagan Traditions*. St. Paul, MN: Llewellyn Publications, 1991.

Janet and Stewart Farrar, *Eight Sabbats for Witches*. Custer, WA: Phoenix Publishing Inc., 1983.

Donna Henes, *Celestially Auspicious Occasions: Seasons, Cycles, and Celebrations*. New York: Perigree Books., 1996.

Chapter 7, Ritual

Renee Beck and Sydney Barbara Metrick, *The Art of Ritual*. Berkeley, CA: Celestial Arts, 1995.

Chapter 8, The Other Side: Expanding Your Awareness

Mary K. Greer, *Tarot for Your Self: A Workbook For Personal Transformation*. N. Hollywood, CA: Newcastle Publications, 1984.

Craig Junjulas, *Psychic Tarot Book*. Stamford, CT: US Games Syst., 1985.

Lawrence LeShan, *How to Meditate*. New York: Bantam Books, 1984.

Chapter 10, Everyday Magic

Thomas Moore, *Care of the Soul*. New York: HarperCollins, 1994.

Hugh Prather, *Notes on How to Live in the World and Still be Happy*. New York: Doubleday, 1986.

Trish Telesco, *The Urban Pagan*. St. Paul, MN: Llewellyn Publications, 1993.

Anything by Alan Watts.

Chapter 11, Community

Chas Clifton, ed., The *Witchcraft Today* series. St. Paul, MN: Llewellyn Publications, 1992–94.

Gerina Dunwich, *The Wicca Source Book*. New Jersey: Citadel Press, 1996.

Wiccan/Pagan Fiction

Marian Zimmer Bradley, *The Mists of Avalon*. New York: Ballantine Books, 1985.

Charles DeLint, *Greenmantle*. (out of print)

Rosemary Edghill, *Speak Daggers to Her*. New York: Forge NYC, 1994.

Stewart Farrar, *The Twelve Maidens*. (out of print)

Katherine Kurtz, *Lammas Night*. New York: Ballantine Books, 1983.

Whitley Streiber, *Cat Magic*. New York: TorBooks, 1987.